ADVANCE PRAISE for

The Zero Dollar Car

"John Ellis looks ahead and connects the dots of the utility of the automobile and the incredible data that is generated from understanding how we use it. His vision and insights will ignite your creativity."

— *Tim Sullivan, managing principal,*
Meyers Research, a Kennedy Wilson Company

"Whether you like it or not, John Ellis tells it like it is."

— *Regina Hopper, former president and CEO,*
ITS America

"In *The Zero Dollar Car*, Ellis shows the power of software and open source, and how they will forever change the transportation world."

— *Jim Zemlin, executive director,*
Linux Foundation

THE
ZERO
DOLLAR
CAR

How the Revolution
in Big Data Will
Change Your Life

JOHN ELLIS

BARLOW BOOKS
fine books for enterprising authors

Library and Archives Canada Cataloguing in Publication data available upon request.

ISBN 978-1-988025-25-4 (hardcover)

Printed in Canada

To Order in Canada:
  Georgetown Publications
  34 Armstrong Avenue, Georgetown, ON L7G 4R9

To Order in the U.S.A.:
  Midpoint Book Sales & Distribution
  27 West 20th Street, Suite 1102, New York, NY 10011

Publisher: Sarah Scott
Project manager: Zoja Popovic
Cover design: Paul Hodgson
Interior design: Kyle Gell Design
Page layout: Kyle Gell Design
Marketing & publicity: Nate Habermeyer/HOWE&WYE

For more information, visit **www.barlowbooks.com**

Barlow Book Publishing Inc.
96 Elm Avenue, Toronto, ON
Canada M4W 1P2

**BARLOW
BOOKS**

For my family

CONTENTS

THE ZERO DOLLAR CAR

W ith the summer season over by the second week of September, 2015, it was quiet around our family's second home on Big Crooked Lake, about two hours east of Chicago in the southwest corner of Michigan. I'd been there all week with my friend Kevin Gutzmer, tearing out the kitchen in preparation for a big remodelling.

A week or so earlier, a guy named Edward Peck had emailed me after coming across my profile on LinkedIn. He was co-founder of the International Auto Finance Network (IAFN) in London, England, and in addition to

putting on his own conferences, he helps other companies stage conferences. This year he was organizing a new
conference for an A-list British technology company called
White Clarke Group, a leader in the automobile captive
finance market, to be held in London in November. The
theme was the digitization of auto financing. The year previous, at Edward's own conference, he'd invited the head
of Jaguar Land Rover's connected car division, the CEO of
Volkswagen financial services, and Hugh Dickerson, the
head of Automotive at Google. For his first conference for
the White Clarke Group, Edward was looking for something
new in a speaker and had noticed that I'd recently spent
close to three years as global technologist at the Ford Motor
Company and head of Ford's software developer program.
He'd watched a couple videos of me giving presentations
for Ford and realized that I knew about the automotive
industry but I was really a software guy. You don't come
across people like that every day, and he thought I might
be a good fit for the conference.

Since leaving Ford a year earlier, I'd taken some time off,
worked on a couple of contracts, and done a few speaking
engagements. Mainly, though, I was trying to figure out
what I was going to do next. A conference in London
sounded inviting, so I agreed to speak with Edward. When
he called me, I was wearing a BlueParrott wireless headset
and had my first-generation Motorola Moto-X phone

tucked in my pocket. It's a good thing we weren't using Skype because I was also wearing work boots, shorts, and a long-sleeved t-shirt and was covered in plaster dust.

Our place on Big Crooked Lake is perched about 75 feet up from the water, the highest point on the lake, and on that warm and sunny day a gentle breeze carried just a hint of autumn through the air. As we talked, I walked in circles around our property, from the side door toward the lake, across the patio, and around the house and back again. While I talked, I often gesticulated with my hands, a John Ellis trademark.

It was the first time Edward and I had ever spoken, so we began with introductions. He then told me a bit about the conference and explained the captive finance market. (Basically, it's the wholly owned financial subsidiaries of automakers, which make loans to customers when they buy cars.) Then Edward asked me if I thought I had anything new or innovative that I could present.

"What do you want to give to this audience?" I asked.

"I'd like to show them the future of technology," he said. "Shake up the status quo a bit. Show them the kind of disruption that might end up happening to the financial market."

"So," I said, "I'll bet something that might challenge the entire financing model would be of interest, even scare them a bit."

I outlined the impending revolution in software—the growing number of vehicle sensors producing previously unimagined volumes of data that would likely upend the auto industry. Remembering a conversation I'd had with the COO of Ford, I told Edward that "companies like Google and Apple are already doing deals to get inside cars for the purpose of acquiring, and then selling, that data. It's possible to imagine a future where the value of that data could change the way consumers buy cars. If the data was monetized, a consumer's data could underwrite the cost of a car. If the price of a car dramatically dropped, that would have to change how it's financed."

Edward, a polite Englishman not given to swearing, nonetheless excitedly said, "Bloody hell, you have this talk ready to go? I want it!"

"Well, not exactly," I said, "but I have all the material and just have to pull it all together."

"Do you have a title for this talk?" Edward asked.

I didn't actually have any material prepared yet, let alone a title. But in a fraction of a second all the times I'd talked about this in the past and all the efforts I'd made to convince Ford and the broader automotive ecosystem to take it seriously came together in a thunderbolt of inspiration.

"The, ah, Zero Dollar Car."

□ □ □

Six days later, Edward sent an email confirming the plans.

From: **Edward Peck** <edwardpeck@asset
financeinternational.com>
Date: Thu, Sep 17, 2015 at 9:11 AM
Subject: FW: Speaker information: White
Clarke Group Summit on Wednesday
November 11, 2015
To: John Ellis <john@ellis-and-associates.
com>

Thank you very much indeed for agreeing
to speak at the White Clarke Group Summit
on Wednesday, November 11, 2015. We are
really looking forward to hearing your
presentation…

Could you let me know whether the details
below are all ok?

Your presentation
You will speak for 30 minutes and then take
questions from the audience.

I am grateful that you will also attend the
rest of the afternoon and the dinner in the
evening so that members can discuss the
topics you raise.

We may also wish you to participate in a
panel discussion.

I am very happy with the proposed outline
we discussed over the phone which explained
by example the value of the data from the
connected car; provided insight into the
value of this using the Google pricing
model you discussed, examines the opportunities for disruptors—and also some likely
responses to it by the industry.

> We would like it to be particularly focused
> on how it might affect the auto finance
> industry (using examples if available)—
> the opportunities and the threats for the
> audience who are C-Level executives from
> the finance divisions of the main global car
> manufacturers (the auto finance captives).
>
> Proposed title:
>
> **"The zero dollar car: why technology compa-
> nies are focusing on the auto industry"**

It was official: I was going to London. Since it was right around the time of our 15th wedding anniversary, I planned on bringing my wife, Karen, so we could celebrate. Now all I had to do was write something worthy of a global conference in the U.K. I didn't have a stock Zero Dollar Car presentation, but I had lots of insights from existing material that I could take. One was a presentation I'd given in 2013 to Mark Fields when he was COO of Ford. (He later became the company's CEO.)

A year earlier, after I'd left Ford, I'd taken on some contracts relating to the automotive industry, including one for the U.S. Department of Transportation, which I was just finishing up. Like everything I was thinking about at the time, it tied into the theme. (It was a third-party program designed to give software developers the tools they needed to develop applications that would collect road- and highway-related data from vehicles and road infrastructure like bridges, intersections, and tollbooths.) I'd also given some talks to venture capital firms. In June, I had delivered the closing keynote for the Leader-2-Leader Builders Conference in San Diego, about business disruption due to digital transformation. In August, I'd spoken at a board dinner hosted by the Intelligent Transportation Society of America, a Washington-based advocacy group. Both had gone well and were paying gigs. But still, I wasn't a professional public speaker by any means.

I was more than a little anxious about it. Would the topic of sensors in cars resonate with the audience? Yes, I thought, but only if I showed them what I was talking about. So I developed a slide illustrating the number of sensors on our modern-day automobiles (see Figure 1).

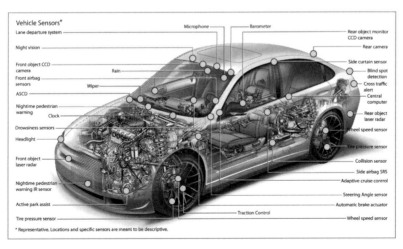

Figure 1 *Vehicle Sensors*

My next concern was whether people would understand exactly why Google and Apple wanted to get their software inside cars. I knew I would have to explain why these big tech companies had spent so much time and money building iOS and Android in the first place.

Apple and Google create hardware and software that provide what industry analyst Richard Windsor calls "digital life services" (that is, email clients, search engines, electronic calendars, music players, and apps). As businesses, they function as large mobile ecosystems, and the more services an ecosystem provides to its members, the less likely it is that a member will move (switch) to a competitor.

These digital life services are also very lucrative. In 2015, Apple earned $20 billion U.S. in gross revenue from its apps alone, which is just under 10% of their total revenue that year. Of that sum, 30% went to Apple (the rest was paid to the app developers).

Google makes money by selling ads and creating technology that enables the rest of us to sell ads. It makes an enormous amount of money from this—$90.3 billion U.S. in 2016—mainly because its deep knowledge of users' online activities enables it to "help advertisers reach users when and where it matters." Anyone who uses a computer knows what that means: If you're searching the internet for advice on your troublesome golf swing, chances are you'll see a Google ad for a golf camp pop up on your screen before you find the tip.

Are Google and Apple planning to accomplish the same feats in cars? They've made the first moves. Think of the screen on the automotive "head unit"—the screen on the dashboard of your car. Right now, each car has a different head unit, with different visuals and functions. They can be tough to understand and use, so Apple and Google have convinced most automakers to switch to the familiar visuals and apps you're used to seeing on your Apple or Android smartphone.

That might be very comforting for people who have trouble figuring out how to use the screen on their new car. But who's the winner here? Will drivers get any financial benefit when the information from their cars is used by Google to sell advertising or by Apple to create new revenue-generating apps? Who will make the money from this data? And what will it do to the auto industry? Will car companies get cut out of the action? If Google and Apple own the dashboard, what will that do to the auto business?

Before leaving for London, I had an opportunity to practice a bit of my presentation. I'd been invited to attend DASH 3.0, a Detroit-based conference bringing together the automotive, advertising, and media communities and focused on the intersection of the internet and the car. My talk was about Apple's and Google's efforts to become embedded infotainment platforms in all cars, and although I didn't directly address the Zero Dollar Car, I covered similar ground. The response from the audience made me feel confident that what I had to say would resonate in London.

Karen and I arrived in London on Sunday, November 8, and spent a couple of days celebrating our anniversary. On Wednesday morning, I got up early and made my way to the Hilton London Canary Wharf, where the conference was taking place. I have a habit of practicing my presentations out loud, thinking about my timing and delivery, so Londoners who saw me walking from my hotel to the Tube or on the train bound for Canary Wharf would have seen a tall guy with a Midwestern American accent talking to himself.

When I arrived at the hotel, I finally met Edward Peck in person. "I'm thankful you made it," he said, as if he'd been worried I might have been a no-show. This was the first conference White Clarke Group was sponsoring so Edward was especially concerned about everything going smoothly. And, he later admitted, my presentation was to him a big part of "it going off right."

I'm not one of those presenters who show up 10 minutes before stepping on stage. I always arrive early, walk around the room, check the sound and audio-video system, and look at the stage. I was also early enough to listen to some of the presentations, which included cyber-crime and how to cater to the auto buying and financing needs of Gens Y and Z, in case I could integrate a few references into my talk.

The term "captive" finance refers to the wholly owned subsidiaries who, in addition to banks, provide loans to buy cars. Ford and Toyota are among the biggest players in this sector. My presentation addressed a pressing question: If the traditional way cars are sold—including the financing—becomes an outdated business model thanks to tech companies like Google and Apple, how would prices for cars be established in the future? That was my theme: What kinds of challenges and opportunities does monetizing the data in connected cars present to manufacturers and the captive finance players?

The conference was crawling with senior executives from the sector, industry experts, and thought leaders, many of whom attended my presentation. As it turned out, I had nothing to worry about.

After I was introduced, I stepped on stage wearing jeans, an open-necked white shirt, and a navy blue blazer. I started my presentation with my first slide (see Figure 2).

Because I was nervous, I spoke quickly and walked around the stage as I spoke. The stage was relatively small, and at one point I nearly fell off the back of the stage as I pointed to the screen. Thankfully, those in attendance seemed riveted by what I had to say and didn't seem to

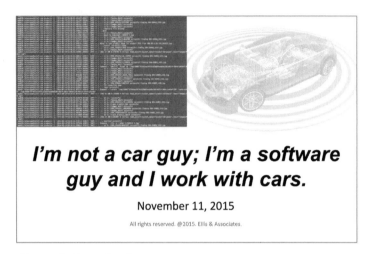

Figure 2 Not a Car Guy

take note. I continued: "Globally, there are 100 million new cars sold every year, and there are in total 1 billion vehicles on the road today. In cash terms, there are projected to be $1 trillion in yearly revenues generated from the auto industry in 2020, so it's big."[1]

However, I continued, it isn't just the number of cars that makes the industry so attractive to technology companies like Google, Apple, Yahoo, Facebook, and Twitter, to name a few. It's the growth of on-board vehicle sensors that

---

1 This is what I said in 2015. Today, there are 1.25 billion vehicles on the road with 88.1 million cars and light commercial vehicles worldwide in 2016, up 4.8% from a year earlier. And in cash terms, the projected value is now closer to $2 trillion in yearly revenues.

generate data that, when combined with location, intentions, and preferences, is incredibly valuable to anyone who can harvest, analyze, and process it. I pointed to a 2013 study by IHS Automotive that estimated the "connected car" would produce approximately $14.5 billion U.S. in revenue from automotive data by 2012.[2]

I explained some basic statistics showing that the nature of driving had changed in the modern world. Long gone are the days when people would get into their cars and drive aimlessly down Main Street or out into the country for no reason other than the sheer novelty of driving. Today, 99.9% of all drives in the U.S. are with intent and purpose—that is, drivers are going from point A to point B for a specific reason. (The percentage is slightly lower in Europe.) And roughly 85% of all drives are what I call "singletons"—the driver is alone and spending roughly 1.5 hours a day in the vehicle, and about 38 hours a year stuck in traffic.

From there I described how each person who participates on the internet has a particular and unique value. Whether you know it or not, Google makes money by selling access to you, the user, to companies seeking to advertise their wares. They do this in a special way: by letting companies

---

2 In 2016, McKinsey issued a report projecting revenue potential as high as $1.5 trillion by 2030.

post their ads on your screen at the same time that you're searching for a service, like help on that errant golf swing. The key is the auction of Google ad words (words and phrases that you use when you search, such as "golf swing help"). Advertisers offer a price for the phrase at a certain time of day, and the one that offers the highest price gets their ad at the top of the screen. That's why you might see an ad for *3D Golf Swing Analysis* on top of the sites you've found for golf tips.

The value of these ad words is determined by auction, and it's possible to calculate the dollar value of any word or phrase at a specific time, say 8:01 a.m. on a Tuesday morning. Knowing this, I decided to find out just how much my friend Kevin generated in ad word revenue for Google over a 3-month period, from June to August 2013. Kevin is a regular Midwestern guy. He has a middle-class income and lives in a house with his wife and two kids. We installed a utility from a company called privacyfix.com (which no longer exists) to assess all of Kevin's Googling on one device, his desktop at home. The privacyfix.com utility then sent data to trefis.com to tell us an estimate for how much Google made in ad words for companies that wanted to post their ads on Kevin's desktop screen. The result: Google was estimated to have made $565 that year in ad money from Kevin's desktop. Kevin made $0. (See Figure 3.)

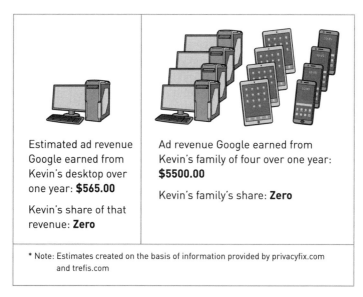

| Estimated ad revenue Google earned from Kevin's desktop over one year: **$565.00**

Kevin's share of that revenue: **Zero** | Ad revenue Google earned from Kevin's family of four over one year: **$5500.00**

Kevin's family's share: **Zero** |

* Note: Estimates created on the basis of information provided by privacyfix.com and trefis.com

Figure 3 *Estimated ad revenue Google earned from Kevin's desktop over one year*

That was strictly for Kevin's desktop. We then estimated what Google would make from his family of four. The result was astounding: Google was estimated to have made $5500 in ad revenue from Kevin and his family across all of their devices. And that was just for Google ads. That didn't include any money that Google made from the data it extracted from Google Analytics, a zero dollar service that companies can use to understand web traffic to their sites. All the data they compile goes to Google, which can be used to make money. Nor did it include any money that

Facebook earned from the information it gathers every time Kevin or his wife "like" something.

If Google can raise $5500 a year from a typical American family's time spent searching for information about brands, consider how valuable that family's data is from a marketer's perspective. Now consider that most drivers get in their cars by themselves with intent and purpose. It's easy to understand why companies like Apple and Google want to get in that car, too: They get a captive audience worth a lot of money.

I presented my next slide: "But what really is the impact?" Thinking of my international audience, I'd designed the following slide to read: "Zero $/£/€ Car."

I could see that everyone was staring with interest but it still wasn't quite sinking in. With the growth of vehicle sensors creating all kinds of data, I told them, tech companies understand that everything—from incoming messages and intelligence gathered by what drivers are saying on their in-car microphones to weather and road conditions—could be sold to, for example, corporations and public utilities.

I provided some examples. In every automobile, there is a sensor connected to a barometer in the engine, and there are other sensors connected to the windshield wipers, headlights, and traction control. Combined, all of these sensors could provide very accurate data about the weather in that car's precise location. So who would be interested in that? Well, the National Oceanic and Atmospheric Administration (NOAA) is a scientific agency with the U.S. Department of Commerce that monitors the weather, including the prediction of serious storms like hurricanes, tornados, and blizzards. If given access, the NOAA could have access to accurate up-to-the-minute weather reports through all the vehicles in every region of the country. Rather than seek federal funding to build another weather station, why not purchase the data from cars?

Cars also include suspension-monitoring sensors that while collecting data on the health of the vehicle's ride could also record every time the vehicle passes over a rough stretch of road in need of repair. This kind of data could be of interest to government agencies who maintain roads and highways.

Think about it. That's *your* data. Imagine if you could sell it for an agreed-upon price and reduce what you pay for the new car you're buying.

"These guys are here. They're smart, sharp, and they know software," I said. "They know analytics, and for them this is a data challenge to be solved." Referring to vehicles, I continued, "The products and services we have sold and transacted in the past, and which we thought had value, are merely the carcasses that carry the *real value*, which is the data."

Automakers, I explained, think they're in the hardware business, building cars and trucks. But today they're actually in the software business, and the sooner they understand that the better off they'll be.

During my presentation I didn't see a single person on their phone, laptop, or other device. I'd left 15 minutes at the end for questions, but after finishing to a solid round of applause, so many people wanted to talk that we had to move outside the room for an additional 45 minutes of discussion.

□ □ □

I knew "Zero Dollar Car" was a clever title for Edward Peck's conference, but I didn't realize that this presentation would launch my speaking career and become the cornerstone of my presentations. In addition to the positive feedback I immediately received from Edward and members of the White Clarke Group, about a month after the presentation Edward posted the video online and I received countless inquiries via LinkedIn and email, including requests for presentations at other conferences and events. It was a little like a YouTube video or a Tweet going viral. My life changed.

One client I worked with in 2016 was Emmis Communications, an Indianapolis-based radio firm. While that job was unrelated to the Zero Dollar Car, the person who hired me had seen the video and was programming a major radio conference in Mexico City. As it happens, I speak fluent Spanish—more on this in Chapter 2—and I told him I could do the presentation in that language. At the Mexico City event, the chairman of Emmis was in the audience and was so impressed with my talk that he contacted the National Association of Broadcasters (NAB) and encouraged them to book me for a keynote address at the annual show in Las Vegas. It turned out that the CTO of NAB was also in the audience. Not only did he support the eventual decision to book me for the keynote, he wanted to personally introduce me to NAB's executive committee. As a result of my presentation on the Zero Dollar Car at the NAB conference in Las Vegas, I was hired to make many more speeches.

In March 2016, I was contacted by BigSpeak, a large California-based speakers' bureau with a database of personalities from business, politics, sports, and film and television who can do anything from give a keynote address to MC a conference. My first engagement for BigSpeak was for WEX, a corporate payments company that does a lot of work in the transportation sector. For the first time, I didn't use the Zero Dollar Car presentation. Instead I talked about the five most important things to consider regarding the future of technology related to transportation and folded the Zero Dollar Car into one of the five.

In April 2016, Edward Peck and I discussed doing a repeat presentation of the Zero Dollar Car at the second annual White Clarke Group conference, to be held again in London. Edward told me that the audience would be a mix of those who had attended my presentation in 2015 and others who would be seeing me for the first time. By this time, I was a more polished presenter, but this situation presented a bit of a dilemma: how to balance between older material that would be repetitive to those who saw me at the first conference (but new to everyone else) and new material?

My solution was to first recap the Zero Dollar Car concept, adding more detail about the growing number of sensors being added to cars all the time. (Many are related to the operation of the engine and many more are for safety reasons—brake sensors, crash sensors, seat belt sensors, anti-lock brake sensors, cameras to help with parking and changing lanes, to name a few.) Then I explained how sensors meant something else to Silicon Valley companies: a rich trove of data waiting to be mined.

I also had a new slide (see Figure 4), and I was quick to point out that it was in fact an outcome of my presentation the year before, which got people's attention. In June 2016, Google published U.S. Patent application number US20160171800, which would allow them to cash in on drivers' personal data. The application reads:

*A method and apparatus for collecting and evaluating
powered vehicle operation utilizing on-board diagnostic
components and location determining components or
systems. The invention creates one or more databases
whereby identifiable behavior or evaluative characteris-
tics can be analyzed or categorized. The evaluation can
include predicting likely future events. The database can
be correlated or evaluated with other databases for a
wide variety of uses.*

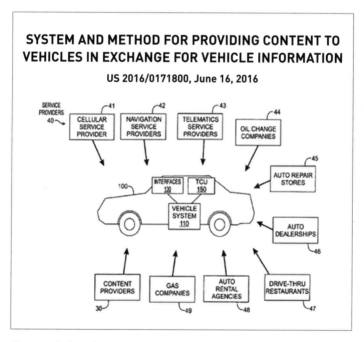

Figure 4 *Google patent application*

This is exactly what I'd talked about in my first presentation, and why at the time I was so certain Google was going to go in this direction. But I should provide some background.

During my last 5 years with Motorola, I was on the leadership team that developed the first-ever third-party developer program for mobile devices. Today, we know this as the "app economy" in which Apple and Google play a significant part. I was also part of a team that built the first-ever Linux-based cell phone. Today we know this as Google's Android or Apple's iOS.[3] Later, when I worked at Ford, I led the team that built SmartDeviceLink, which the auto industry at the time didn't embrace. But Google and Apple did, and today we know this as Google's Android Auto and Apple's CarPlay. That's why I've jokingly said "If you want to know what Google and Apple are going to do, just follow me because *they* seem to be following me." It got a laugh in 2015, but now everyone could see I wasn't kidding.

In sum, automakers have the potential to control how and when third parties get vehicle data, but do they understand how valuable it is and will they act? I'm skeptical,

3 I realize iOS is built on top of BSD, which is not Linux. When speaking publicly, I call out the fact that Motorola was the first to take an open source operating system (Linux) and put it on a phone. Apple did the same with BSD (following in the footsteps left by Motorola and its Linux efforts).

since my team and I developed the technology to do this when I was at Ford and then convinced Ford to open source it and give it to the other automakers. (The other automakers said "No, thanks" and all of them began embracing Google and Apple, who implemented the technology themselves.)

So what was my message for the crowd at this captive finance conference, all of whom are people who understand how to build business models based on data and know how to collaborate with other companies within the automotive industry? If they played a new, more proactive role with product development teams, they could monetize the data and own new sources of revenue. If they could do that, I told them, they would become "KARS"—Kick Ass Rock Stars.

My presentation was a hit.

Of course, that's the captive finance sector, another group of corporate executives looking to make money off consumer data. The dream of the Zero Dollar Car was that *consumers* could benefit from the loss of their personal data by getting a vehicle at a much-reduced price. Let me break it down for you.

Imagine that you're buying a $40,000 U.S. car. Say you want to reduce the price of that car by agreeing to sell the information generated by six sensors: traction control, headlights, clock, wipers, rain, and barometer. If you could sell those weather sensors for an agreed-upon lifetime price, let's say $3000, that would reduce the price of the car to $37,000.

Cars also contain suspension-monitoring sensors that, while providing information on the health of the vehicle's ride, could also record every time the vehicle passes over a rough stretch of road in need of repair. This data is potentially of interest to government agencies who maintain roads and highways. Now imagine that you could sell the suspension-monitoring sensors to a government agency for, let's say, another $2000 lifetime price. That would reduce the price of the car you're buying to $35,000.

Almost every modern-day car contains a microphone. Imagine giving permission to Google to monitor what is being said in the vehicle to better help with navigation or searching for that perfect place to eat. If you could sell your voice data to Google for a $5000 lifetime price, that would reduce the price of the vehicle to $30,000. And what about handing over the information from sensors that detect speed and from car cameras? That might be valuable traffic information that could cut another $2000 off the purchase price of your car.

In theory, if you sold the data being generated from several more sensors, you could dramatically reduce the price of your $40,000 car. Now imagine what could happen in the future, when there are lots more sensors, and companies like Apple and Google figure out new ways to package the data coming out of those cars—especially self-driving cars that leave riders plenty of time to read and shop and play on their portables or phones. The value of that data could end up being equal to or more than the purchase price of a car. It could be a data bonanza. Who would be the winner? If it's you, the driver, you could have a car that effectively costs you zero—the Zero Dollar Car (see Figure 5).

Is that feasible? I think it will be in the near future—but only if consumers understand the real dollar value of the

Base Price for Car:	$40,000.00
Subtract payments for data generated by sensors:	
Weather:	$3,000.00
Suspension:	$2,000.00
In-car microphone:	$5,000.00
Traffic (speed, cameras):	$2,000.00
Subtotal:	$28,000.00
Subtract more data from other sensors that companies (like retailers or insurance companies) want to buy:	$28,000.00
Upfront payment by driver for $40,000.00 car:	**Zero**
Note: Estimates created by John Ellis	

Figure 5 *The zero dollar car*

data generated by the cars they drive and the devices they use. And only if they have the power to decide whether they want to make this bargain.

□ □ □

While the Zero Dollar Car is still part of what I do, I've broadened my focus. Now I market myself as a technologist and futurist who can talk in general about big data and the Internet of Things (IoT), with an emphasis on transportation and autonomy.

The car, though, was a starting point for me. Combined with what I'd learned working for years on cellular infrastructure networks at Motorola Inc., I'd been at ground zero of what, today, we call the IoT. How will the revolution in big data change our lives? That was something I understood and about which I was ready to educate people.

2

WHO IS
JOHN ELLIS?

The Zero Dollar Car is really about data, technology, privacy, and where it's taking our lives. There's no shortage of experts out there telling you where things are going and what you should think about it, but how do you know what to believe and who to trust? I suggest getting to know more about anyone who puts himself or herself forward as an "expert," let alone a "futurist."

So who is John Ellis?

The eldest of two boys, my dad, John Charles Ellis, was born and raised in Chicago. Dad worked for the city as an operating engineer in charge of big boilers, but he was what you'd call a blue-collar academic. He was constantly educating himself. When he got called up for military service during the Vietnam War, he was assigned to the Green Berets and ended up in Okinawa as an instructor to the Special Forces. Back home in Chicago, he went back to school and became a master certified instructor for all operating engineers in the city. During the summers, he taught a class on operating engineer principles at the University of Wisconsin-Milwaukee's Extension School of Engineering. As if that wasn't enough, he went to night school and earned his master's degree in public administration from the Illinois Institute of Technology.

Dad grew up in what's currently known as the Methodist Church, with a strong belief in getting stuff done. He wasn't overly religious, but he understood the importance of believing in something. His brother, my uncle Tom, was deployed to Vietnam three times, and spent a period of time imprisoned in a POW camp. I remember the stories they shared. My uncle would say to my dad, "I have seen hell, and when you've been in hell you want to believe there's something more." Sitting in a corner and listening intently, I thought that was a powerful statement.

When I was growing up, Dad was always wrenchin'. On weekends, if he wasn't fixing our appliances—especially the washing machine, dryer, or furnace—he was doing repair work for friends or neighbors, and he'd always take me along to help. By the age of six or seven, I knew the difference between a socket wrench and a crescent wrench. I would hand the correct tool to my dad when he was curled into tight, uncomfortable positions underneath or behind a machine. I knew how to replace a dryer belt and a thermal coupler by the time I was eight. I remember him telling me, "Don't be afraid to take something apart. You'll figure out how to put it back together. On the off chance you can't, you'll be an engineer and can afford to buy a new one."

Coincidentally, my dad grew up next door to my mom. Anne Marie Ellis (née Clifford) was one of three children. Her mother was an office worker at the Chicago Park District, and her father was a senior clerk for City of Chicago Streets and Sanitation. They lived in the tightly knit St. Sabina Parish on the south side of Chicago and attended St. Sabina Catholic Church. She went to Chicago Teachers College and soon after began teaching elementary school. She later trained teachers but after she married my dad and they started a family, she decided to stay home and focus on what, as a parent myself, I know to be the toughest job.

The eldest of six children, I have three sisters (Eileen, Elizabeth, and Annemarie) and two brothers (Tom and Michael). Chicago's public school system was pretty poor back in the early 1970s, so even though it was a financial sacrifice, my parents sent all of us to Catholic grammar school and high school. This decision was in no small part due to my mom's own Catholic education first at St. Sabina grammar school and then at the Academy of Our Lady High School.

Dad worked a lot of part-time jobs to earn extra income so mom was the driving force in our family: the disciplinarian and the shoulder we all cried on, the person who taught us good study habits as well as how to balance a check book. When I was 18, she finally had an opportunity to resume the career she loved, at a public school a few blocks from our home, and she continued teaching until she was nearly 70.

Music was a big part of our family life. Dad played accordion as a child and picked up piano as well. In high school he played trombone, and somewhere along the way he learned guitar, too. All six of us kids took music lessons and played instruments. I started piano lessons in the first grade, and then took up the trumpet in fourth grade. Going into my freshman year at high school, I was a trumpet player in band and trying out for basketball. I remember having one of my first adult conversations with my parents about that. My mother, for whom academic success was hugely important, told me I couldn't possibly pass all my courses if I was in the band, taking piano lessons, and playing basketball on the team. I told them that if I made the team I wanted to quit piano. Dad agreed, but reminded me that I would have to live with that choice. I made the team, and although I don't have very many regrets today, one of them is that after studying piano so intensely, I stopped playing (though I continued to play the trumpet all the way through college).

Dad worked a lot, but whenever he was around I spent a lot of time with him. He was a true engineer: He loved to tinker and loved new gadgets. He once built a stereo system from scratch and would play his favorites—big band music like Woody Herman, and brass favorites like Herb Alpert and the Tijuana Brass. Ours was the first house in the neighborhood to have new technology. I remember being in fourth grade when my dad brought home Pong, that early table-tennis video game that you plugged into a TV. We had the first VCR in the neighborhood, too. Around 1983 he bought a home computer, a Toshiba T100 running the old CP/M operating system that came with a thick manual. (What's a "file system"? We'd thumb through the pages looking it up. Oh, DIR means "directory...")

But that wasn't my first exposure to a computer. A few years earlier, when I was in seventh grade, I was selected as one of three kids to be taken to a business somewhere in downtown Chicago to see an IBM computer. I remember that the computer was in a room by itself with locked doors, and we were able to feed numbered punch cards into its slots. Even then I sensed that I was looking at the future. When I was a junior in high school, I took my first programming class and felt a real affinity for computing. My school had a PDP 7 and a VAX 11/780. I only mention these because they were both made by Digital Equipment Corporation (DEC), which at that time owned the growing 32-bit minicomputer market.

Later in life and early in my career, I discovered one of the best books on technology I've ever read: journalist Tracy Kidder's *The Soul of a New Machine*. It tells the story of two design teams within Data General Corporation, each trying to come up with a new minicomputer to compete with DEC's VAX 11/780. What really struck me was how Kidder made circuit boards, micro sequencers, and Boolean algebra seem impossibly romantic, especially to a young guy like me. I was enamored with the idea that people would buy into the ritual of "signing up"—going full-out, 24/7, without regard for a personal life—because they weren't just building a machine, they were creating a revolutionary new kind of art.

I was a better-than-average student, always good at math. Overall, I scored consistent As and Bs. (In our home, C was not an acceptable grade.) One thing I did learn over time, and certainly by the time I was in university, is that I'm a "big pattern" guy. It comes from studying math and computer science, yes, but even learning a language is all about patterns. What I've learned about myself is that when I see a problem, I analyze it quickly. I'm either very close or 100% right or I'm completely wrong. No in-between. So I've learned to evaluate things fast and whatever I decide, I jump all over it. As an approach, it's served me well.

I remember taking my first Spanish class as a freshman in Marist High School, an all-boys Catholic high school I attended in 1981. I was immediately hooked. Which was ironic. You see, I had originally wanted to study French. Before starting at Marist, my parents told me I had to choose a language: Spanish, French, or German. Not knowing the pros or cons of any of them, I decided to investigate each language. It seemed to me that the landscapes and people showcased in the French-language recruitment literature were exotic, beautiful, and intriguing. Armed with this information, I informed my parents I was going to study French.

My dad was not impressed. He explained why French and German were impractical for someone growing up on the south side of Chicago. Since there was a strong and ever-present Latin—and particularly Mexican—community within the city, he decided I was going to study Spanish. And I'm glad I did.

During my first Spanish lesson I was more excited than I had anticipated. I liked the idea that learning a language would separate me from the folks I'd grown up with, and although I couldn't explain exactly why, I also sensed the opportunities that speaking a second language might bring. After that first class, I recall proudly saying to my mom, "*Me llamo John.*" ("My name is John.")

I loved studying Spanish, but I had no idea what it was going to mean to my career in the not-too-distant future.

The Catholic high school I attended had a sister school in Mexico. One day, Brother Gerard Brereton told us an exchange student was coming whose parents wanted him to stay with a freshman family. I asked my parents if we could be his host family and they agreed. I remember meeting Ricardo Bayón Lira at the O'Hare Airport in April 1982. My father left work early, and we arrived in time to meet Ricardo as he passed through immigration. Ricardo was a freshman but nearly a year younger than me, and I was struck by the smell of his cologne and how it was all a little awkward at first as we shook hands and I tried, with my very limited Spanish, to speak to him.

Ricardo stayed with us for seven weeks, and it was during this time that I learned the joy of sharing my culture and transcending national boundaries. By the time Ricardo returned to Mexico, I felt like I had another brother. (He lives in the U.S. today; I'm godfather to Ricky, his first-born, and he's godfather to my son, John.) For years we exchanged letters and, even though long-distance phone calls were expensive back then, my parents allowed me one call a month so we could stay in touch (they liked Ricardo, too).

In the spring of 1984, my junior year, Ricardo's family invited me to spend a few weeks with them in Toluca, Mexico. With the blessing of my high school, I went on an incredible four-week adventure. I'd go to school with Ricardo and to church with the Bayón family, who treated me like one of the family. (His mom and dad introduced me as *mi hijo*—"my son"). I may not have been fluent in Spanish by the time I returned to Chicago, but I was well on the way and determined to make the most of the last year of the Spanish program at my high school.

A year later, in my senior year, Ricardo called to ask a favor. He said his cousin, Arturo Peña, was a student at the St. John Military Academy in Delafield, Wisconsin, and he wondered if my family would consider letting him spend Easter break with us. We were happy to, of course, and with my Spanish much improved I could talk to Arturo with ease. Little did I know then how far Arturo was going to go.

With high-school graduation on the horizon, my mom (like all good Catholic moms) wanted me to go to the University of Notre Dame. We went to have a look and, of course, were impressed. But my uncle said I should take a look at Valparaiso University, where two of my older cousins had considered going (and which we would pass on our way home from our Notre Dame visit). Commonly known as Valpo or VU, it's a private Lutheran university in Valparaiso, Indiana, that at that time enrolled about 4000 students from more than 50 countries. I was impressed. It's predominately an undergraduate, liberal arts college and, because it didn't have the usual obsession with being a research institution, you were taught by senior professors, not teaching assistants. What really swayed me was their attitude toward student travel. My experience in Mexico had convinced me that I wanted to spend more time abroad. At the time, Notre Dame didn't have a program that accommodated travel for engineering students but Valpo encouraged it.

As I was applying to VU, I remember my dad telling me the price would be the same whether I took 12 credit hours a semester or 21. I understood what he was getting at—make the most of my time in university—so I signed up for 21 credit hours every semester (and as many credits as I could take in the summer) even though it meant I would be studying much of the time.

□ □ □

When I started high school I thought I would probably become a mechanical engineer, like my dad. Then I got very excited by computer programming and electronics and decided that's what I wanted to do. But one day a religious brother came to our class and talked to us about "the calling." If you've ever been awake at night wondering about, yearning for, or questioning the meaning of life, he said, you might want to consider a religious calling, and we encourage you to spend time with us. I was fascinated by that; it really touched me. So I arrived at VU with the expectation that not only would I become a priest, but also that I would use my Spanish and become a missionary. Some people who know me today might hear that and think I was putting on an act, that I was insincere, but at the time I was absolutely serious. Over my 5 years at university, I went regularly to the Newman Center, the Catholic organization on campus, where I attended mass and went on retreats to build homes for the poor.

I had some college credits after doing well on a college-level Advanced Placement computer science class in high school. I wished there had been an Advanced Placement for Spanish, too, but alas, my high school did not have such a course. So during my first week at Valpo, maybe endowed with a little bit too much self-confidence for someone in their first week of university, I went to talk to the chair of the Spanish department. "I don't have Advanced Placement," I said, "but if I can get at least a B on the third semester final exam that you gave last year, will you give me the credits for the three semesters?" She looked skeptical but let me do it. To her surprise, I scored a B+ and was allowed to start in fourth semester Spanish as well as receive credits for three college Spanish classes.

In my sophomore year, I applied for VU's semester abroad program. Along with some classmates, I went to the University of the Americas in Cholula, Mexico, to study Spanish and even take some engineering classes in Spanish. There I met a phenomenal teacher named Sally Ochoa, who was in charge of the Valpo students while they were in Mexico. She taught me how to recognize patterns in language. Once you understand the patterns, you can trust your gut instinct and put yourself out there, knowing that you'll be right more often than you're wrong. (But you also need to know enough to back off when you realize you're wrong.)

Patterns also figured in an influential book I later studied: Douglas Hofstadter's *Gödel, Escher, Bach: An Eternal Golden Braid*, which is a meditation on creativity and how the human mind works told through the Austrian mathematician Kurt Gödel, classical composer Johann Sebastian Bach, and Dutch artist M.C. Escher. It's a seminal text for those in the tech field, and to this day I still have my dog-eared, marked-up copy. (My wife once said "You should get rid of that old book." My response: "No, no, *do not* throw that book away!") From *Gödel, Escher, Bach* I realized that I had developed big pattern thinking thanks to my background in music, mathematics, and language.

An overview of that book on Amazon.com reads: "Everything is a symbol, and symbols can combine to form patterns. Patterns are beautiful and revelatory of larger truths … this book shows … more clearly than most any other, what it means to see symbols and patterns where others see only the universe." That book helped me understand what I believe is my fundamental skill set: the ability to "see symbols and patterns where others see only the universe."

What I learned from Sally Ochoa and from that book would prove to be important in years to come.

When I wasn't taking classes, I was with Ricardo and his family. Arturo lived near Ricardo's family in Toluca, so I spent time with Arturo, too, and met his brother, Enrique, along with the rest of the family. Sometimes Enrique gave me a ride back into Mexico City, where I would catch the bus back to Cholula. We got along well, and I remember thinking he'd be going places because he was a really smart guy. (Today you know him as Enrique Peña Nieto, the president of Mexico.)

A decade or so ago, I met a Spanish teacher at my local public high school while watching my children swim. He invited me in for a "language day" to share my thoughts with the students on studying a foreign language. It went over so well that I go back every year. This is my message to the students:

> *In 1981, I was a blue-collar Irish Catholic kid living in a neighborhood on the south side of Chicago surrounded by people just like me. Learning another language opened so many doors. When you learn a new language, you're also learning a new culture. It teaches you empathy, and you discover that people who speak a different language and may live in a different part of the world are just the same as you. It gave me many fascinating work opportunities, too, including the opportunity to act as a translator at the Olympics. And today I know the President of Mexico.*

◻ ◻ ◻

At the beginning of my fourth year at Valpo, I went to see an academic counselor. I told her that I wasn't sure I was ready to graduate, but it was my senior year so we might as well get this process started. She looked at my records and told me that I had enough credit hours for two degrees. "If we tweaked your course work a little, and you stayed another year, you could graduate with three degrees," she said. I thought about that. She wasn't talking about a major, where you can graduate with a double major in two areas of study but it's still only one degree.

I could actually end up with 3 degrees in 5 years. And it meant that I could stay in the college environment for another year.

So I did. I graduated in 1990 with a Bachelor of Science in computer science, a Bachelor of Science in math, and a Bachelor of Arts in Spanish. The first and, to this day, the only time that's happened in the history of the university.

During that final year of university, I still intended to become a priest immediately upon graduation—until I had some long conversations with my spiritual adviser. He said, "You'll make a great priest, but you'll be a better priest if you get some life experience. And college isn't life experience. You should pursue a professional life. Stay in touch with us, and when the time is right we'll figure it out."

He could see how much I loved the work I'd been doing in computer science, a growing field with many opportunities. And he was right. If I was ever going to become a priest, and perhaps one day teach at VU or another university, or even do missionary work in Latin America, I'd be better off with some life experience.

So I went to the university's career office and talked to Sandy McGuigan, the wife of the man who coordinated my exchange trip to Mexico a couple of years earlier. She told me to write a resumé—explaining how to structure it and instructing me to make it no longer than one page—and then let her see it. When I did, it was two pages long. "No, John," she said, "it has to be one page." "Why? Is it a law? I have diverse experience, and it needs to be two pages." In the end, she relented.

A month or so later, early in the morning, Sandy called me at the fraternity house. She had been working the last two years to get Motorola Inc. onto the campus for interviews with students, and they had finally said yes. She told me she had an open spot in her calendar that afternoon for the Motorola recruiter, and there was no way she was going to let that happen. "Be in my office at 2:00 this afternoon for an interview," she said, reminding me that I owed her big-time for all the hassling over my resumé.

The Motorola representative was a very nice woman. "So, why do you want to join Motorola?" she asked.

Being the cocky 22-year-old that I was, and not having any better answer, I said, "You know what? I have no idea about Motorola, other than that I used your company's semiconductor chip for part of my senior project. I'm here because the counselor needed someone to sit in this seat at this time. Maybe I should ask you, why should I want to join Motorola?"

Later I thought, Well, Ellis, you blew that. There's no way they're going to hire you. But I also consoled myself: I'd had no time to prepare, and if I'd pretended I knew anything about Motorola the recruiter would have known

I was bullshitting. Better to be honest. And, in fairness to the recruiter, she told me exactly why I should want to work at Motorola. The look on my face probably read "Wow, that's cool," because at one point the recruiter smiled and said, "Yeah, that's what we do. We build cool stuff."

At the time, Motorola was a $9.6 billion U.S. provider of electronic equipment, systems, and services for international markets. Its products included two-way radios, pagers, cell phones, semiconductors, and electronics for industry, especially the automotive and aerospace sectors. It supplied the guts for many brand-name personal computers. Motorola had designed a cellular phone for cars, but it was big and heavy, using so much power that it only worked when the engine was running. In the mid-70s, Dr. Martin Cooper led a team at Motorola that developed the DynaTAC 8000x, the first commercially available cell phone small enough to be carried around. By today's standards, it was far from small: it weighed 28 ounces and stood 10 inches high (not including its antennae). It was a brick. And it offered only 30 minutes' talk time after a 10-hour charge. Priced at several thousand dollars, it was mainly a status symbol for the very wealthy. As we now know, all that was soon to change.

According to Motorola's 1989 annual report, "The 1980s may be remembered as the decade of personal computing, but the 1990s may well be the decade of personal communicating... As we move to an all-digital world, which allows transmission of data and images along with voice, it's not hard to imagine turning a personal telephone into a computer terminal and video device."

Yeah, I thought, that does sound like a cool place.

3

THE MOTOROLA YEARS

M uch to my surprise, in January 1990, I received a
letter offering me an on-site interview at Motorola
in the newly formed cellular division. I remember the date
of the interview because it was the day after Valentine's
Day: February 15. The distance from Valpo to Motorola's
cellular infrastructure division's head office in Arlington
Heights, northwest of Chicago, was about 90 miles. I rented
a car and booked a hotel room so I could wake up and go
directly to my morning appointment. It's a good thing
I did. A huge snowstorm hit the region on Valentine's

Day, with whiteout conditions. What should have been a
2-hour drive took me nearly 8 hours. I arrived exhausted
and, to be honest, concerned about the interview. I'd been
flippant at that initial meeting with the Motorola representative, but since then I'd figured out that working for
them would be very cool, just right for me.

One of the most prestigious corporations in America,
Motorola began in Chicago in 1928 as the Galvin
Manufacturing Corporation and was a pioneer in radio
communications, producing the first mass-market dashboard car radio, installed in a Studebaker, in 1930. That
year it created a new brand name by combining "motor"
(motorcar) with "ola" (from Victrola, the name of a popular gramophone), and a decade later officially adopted it
as its corporate name. Over the years, the company built
two-way radio devices for the military, police, fire departments, ambulances, and taxis, as well as making consumer
products like home radios and, later, televisions. In 1940,
it invented the world's first walkie-talkie—the Handie-
Talkie—for the U.S. military, and 6 years later Motorola
equipment carried the first calls on a radio-telephone
installed in a car. When transistors came on the scene in
the 1950s, Motorola began using them in its own products and supplying them to other companies. In 1969,
when Neil Armstrong stood on the surface of the moon
and said "One small step for a man, one giant leap for

mankind," he was using a Motorola transceiver. By the 1980s, Motorola's microprocessors were powering computers made by Apple, Hewlett-Packard, Sun Microsystems, and others. Long before the days when cell phones would be in the hands of almost everyone, Motorola was in the business of mobile communications and by the time I was hired, everyone from business executives to politicians to government officials (in the U.S. and abroad) wanted to talk to Motorola.

Talk about star talent. Marty Cooper, the guy who invented the first cell phone, was still working at Motorola at the time. The engineers who designed the telecommunications for Apollo 11 were still there. It was arguably the hottest company in America, and I wanted to be part of it.

When I arrived at the Motorola campus for my 8:00 a.m. interview with HR, the entire place was practically deserted. The snowfall the previous night was so heavy that employees either couldn't make it to the office or elected to stay home. The HR representative told me that half the people who were to be there for my interview weren't coming to work, although he pointed out that the fact that I showed up would make me look good. (To this day, my mother likes to tease me, saying that's the only reason I got the job.) A month later, Motorola hired me in its Cellular Infrastructure Division, the part of the company that built switches and base stations, the infrastructure backbone of the growing cellular network, at a salary of $32,600.

After graduating from Valparaiso University, and knowing I had a job waiting for me at Motorola, I spent a couple of months traveling around Mexico with Ricardo, having a good time and becoming even more comfortable speaking Spanish. I returned to Chicago and started work on July 30, 1990.

My parents had divorced in 1989, which was tough on everyone, especially my youngest siblings. I was living at my mom's house, which happened to be about 45 miles from the Motorola offices. My first day at work started with a few hours of "on-boarding" (the classic first-day orientation where you're given a tour of the office, introduced to key people, complete the formal paperwork, etc.). Afterwards, I met my escort for the day. He led me from the administrative area of the company to the engineering area, the home of the cellular infrastructure division. It had just been relocated to a newly renovated building that had originally been part of Shure Brothers, Inc., the company famous for its phonograph cartridges and, especially, microphones and sound systems (they were used throughout the entertainment industry; in fact, during Elvis Presley's early days on-stage, he used Shure mics). I was shown to my cubicle, where I found a brand-new Sun 3 workstation.

(A UNIX system produced by Sun Microsystems, it used Motorola's then state-of-the-art 68020 microprocessor.) I was given my login credentials and introduced to my team and our team leader.

The first few weeks were a blur of meetings, introductory courses on cellular network design, the principles of telephone queuing theory, radio theory, and other arcane industry intelligence, as well as spending time with the IT crew learning how to customize my Sun3 machine. During this initial period with the company, I figured out how best to learn the significant amount of information needed to develop and deploy what would become one of the world's most important communication systems, including the basic third-party test and verification equipment used during the installation and maintenance of the equipment in the field.

To avoid driving in rush hour, I usually arrived at the office between 6:00 and 6:30 a.m., and left close to 7:00 p.m. That gave me a lot of time to spend in the lab learning how to use the Motorola products and test equipment as well as how the network sub-systems worked. I was applying the lessons I'd learned from my father about engineering principles and how to study a thing from the inside out to figure out how it worked. My goal each day was to generate a list of questions about what I'd seen or heard that I would later take to the older, veteran engineers, some of whom became mentors, who would explain it all to me. That was the best education I could get.

I'm sure everyone has seen pictures of an old-fashioned switchboard, with an operator plugging and unplugging cables to connect callers. That basic system was replaced by electromechanical hardware that did the job of operators. By the time I got to Motorola, a cellular telephone switching system operated on a huge scale, with powerful computers managing the radio base stations into which phone calls were routed. In telecommunications, an electronic switching system is used to interconnect telephone circuits. A cell phone communicates wirelessly with a base station connected to a mobile switch. That switch, which might control hundreds of base stations, would connect the cell signal either to another mobile switch or to the landline system. The switch is the heart of the network—or, as I used to say to my phone hardware colleagues, "Without a switch, the phone is just an expensive paperweight."

By the end of the 80s, Motorola was a global supplier of cell phones and had recognized an opportunity in the marketplace outside North America. In many countries, especially emerging nations, the expense of creating, or upgrading, an inefficient landline system was so great that governments decided to move directly to installing cellular networks. And Motorola, whose Micro TAC flip phone was already a leading product in Europe, understood that populations would adopt cell phones so long as there was an infrastructure and service available, both of which Motorola could supply.

All that time in the lab paid off, both in my growing knowledge and in how I was regarded by my superiors. Within a few months of my starting at the company, Motorola was selecting people for a team being sent to Barcelona, Spain. They needed a switch engineer, and although there were probably better switch engineers than me, I'd worked so hard that I was good enough and, combined with my fluency in Spanish, was seen as an ideal candidate.

If I'd acquired a working knowledge of our infrastructure—the switches and base stations—for what was then an analog phone system, boy, I learned a lot in Spain. Motorola liked to hire people who had been doing electronics in the military so I worked with a top engineering team in Barcelona. It didn't take me long to understand that the reality of installing and maintaining our equipment in the field wasn't necessarily the same as instructions from our head office. These guys would say to me, "John, we get that's what the document says, but that's not what the fuck we're gonna do." And they always showed me why, to work in the field, it had to be adapted in a different way.

I learned other, more basic, life lessons, too. On my third day we found a nice local bar and after our drinks, the field engineers left a $200 U.S. tip for Fernando, our waiter.

"What the hell are you doing?" I asked.

"You'll see," they said, and continued to leave big tips the next couple of weeknights, too.

That Saturday, we went to the bar at around 9:00 p.m. and it was jam-packed. One of the engineers said to me, "Ellis, stand on your tiptoes in the doorway and get Fernando's attention." When he saw me, I signaled that there were five of us. A few minutes later he found us a table and our first few drinks were on the house. Fernando's behavior would continue like this for the duration of our 6-week visit. No matter how crowded the bar, whenever we showed up we were immediately seated and the first few rounds were on the house. The engineering guys, who had lived around the world, taught me that you establish yourself with the staff at your favorite bar or restaurant as foreigners who aren't going to take advantage of the locals and you quickly become accepted as a "regular." The same was true of the field engineers themselves. I learned that if I took care of them, they'd take care of me.

Pretty soon I'd developed a reputation. *If you've got a problem and need someone in a Spanish-speaking country, ask for Ellis.* In those early years, in addition to trips back and forth to Spain, I was servicing the Latin American markets where Motorola was installing cellular infrastructure. (Spanish truly was my trump card. Here I was, in my mid-20s, traveling all over the world with a company credit card.)

I remember being in Caracas, Venezuela, in 1991. There were problems that the engineers in the U.S. couldn't solve. I was pretty sure I'd figured out what was happening, and suggested the company send me there for a few weeks to troubleshoot and validate my hypothesis. For me to be successful, the field engineers in Caracas were going to have to do a lot of work and coordinate with me on a daily basis. That meant they had to at least trust me, if not like me, and that isn't always easy when you're the guy from the head office being parachuted in. So I met with my field engineering team at a Caracas restaurant, opened a $2000 U.S. tab for dinner and drinks, and explained what I wanted. Guess what? Remember that idea of "signing up," from Tracy Kidder's book, *The Soul of a New Machine*? Well, they all got on board and worked crazy hours for weeks until we fixed the problem. Then I threw a close-out party before I flew back to the States.

Meanwhile, I'd demonstrated a flair for writing reports that were both detailed and factual, which management liked. And I knew how to communicate and educate, which I'd picked up from my mother and father. Whenever there was a tough job, I often got the call. I'd figured out that angry customers wanted to be heard and acknowledged. I'd say, "Listen, I get that you're pissed off and frustrated, and it probably is my company's fault. I'm sorry. But in order to do my job and make things right, I need you to help me. So let's walk this journey together..."

By the end of it, we were usually drinking buddies.

I knew I was both smart and quick, which means I had to learn the fine line between confidence and arrogance. My ability to see the big picture and adeptness at pattern recognition meant that I often instantly saw the solution to a problem. What I learned, though, was that even if my decision wouldn't change over the next half hour or so, I needed to ask the customer questions, give them an opportunity to explain, so they could feel they were part of the process. The same is true with my teams. That subtle part of leadership can be an Achilles heel for many leaders.

During one of my extended trips to Spain, I met a woman named Maria Teresa who helped me get a gig as a volunteer Spanish translator at the 1992 Barcelona Olympics. (I could never have done it without the confidence instilled in me by that Spanish teacher, Sally Ochoa, who taught me to trust my instincts.) That meant taking more than 2 months off work, but I negotiated a deal with Motorola. A hiring freeze was on so my manager quietly arranged for me to continue on the payroll for 8.5 weeks and repay the company in overtime when I was back. I was able to arrange housing in a crash pad with some flight attendants I'd met while working there and, because it was the first year the NBA allowed its players to compete, I met a number of the first-ever Dream Team, including Michael Jordan, Scottie Pippin, Clyde Drexler, and John Paxson. It was an amazing experience I'll always remember.

During my early years at Motorola, I was promoted twice. I learned that Bob Galvin, the son of the founder who was then chairman of Motorola, endorsed higher education and professional development. Some of my colleagues were doing their master's degree at the Illinois Institute of Technology, commonly referred to as IIT, and the company was paying for it. I signed up and, in January 1993, began working on my master's in computer science. IIT had set up a satellite campus at Motorola, with a microwave feed and an interactive video hook-up. Motorola students would sit in Motorola training offices while the classes were broadcast live. There was a phone in the room, and students could use that to speak directly to the professor and students in the campus classroom. In addition to working full time, I was able to take three courses in each of the spring, summer, and fall semesters, and fast-track through the program.

In the early fall of 1993, I learned that some of the company's best and brightest were being recruited to work in China (the newest market for Motorola), and a mentor suggested I apply. I was sent overseas for a preliminary visit, and when I returned the company offered me a position there for 2 years.

When Motorola entered China in 1987, opening an office in Beijing using the name Motorola China Electronics Ltd., it was the only provider of network equipment and analog cell phones in the country, giving it strong brand recognition. In 1992, just three years after Tiananmen Square, it established a $120 million facility in Tianjin, a large industrial city in northern China, to produce cell phones, pagers, two-way radios, semiconductors, automotive electronics, telecom gear, and other products. Motorola was, at the time, among the biggest and most successful foreign companies operating in China.

When I went to my IIT adviser to let them know of the foreign assignment, I was told I could put my graduate studies on hold—you had 5 years to complete the program—but I knew the expiration date was the least of my problems. Imagine trying to write a master's exam when you've been away from your studies for several years. I asked if I could take the exam before I left for China. Understandably, their first reaction was skepticism. I'm sure they were thinking, *Dude, you've only been in the program for 9 months and you want to write the exam?* But the prerequisite to writing the exam was having enough diversification of course work, and because I'd nearly completed nine courses I could make a legitimate claim. The faculty member responsible for administering the master's exam process said if I wanted to try, I could. "However," he said, "you only get a total of three chances. Fail three times and you fail the program and must leave the university." Furthermore, to pass the exam you needed to correctly answer four out of the five questions. I knew it would be a challenge, but I joined a study group with four Motorola employees who'd been doing the master's program for 3 years and were preparing to write the exam.

I began to realize that my behavior fit a pattern, which can be summarized as "I don't accept the status quo": During those first days at Valparaiso, convincing the chair of the Spanish department to let me write the third semester final exam and leap-frog ahead to Spanish 4. Later refusing to accept the career office's one-page resumé requirement, which indirectly led to the Motorola interview. Insisting on writing the Master of Computer Science exam after only 9 months in the program. It would happen many more times in the coming years, enough that I would call it my *modus operandi:* refusing to accept the constraints I'm facing, rewriting the rules.

I'm a "big picture" thinker.

While learning about networks and mobile technology generally at Motorola, I realized that many of my colleagues saw things in discrete units: a single switch or base station or phone. I, however, instantly understood the interconnectedness of it all, what we call an ecosystem or what is in fact now understood as the Internet of Things (IoT). Back in the early 90s, though, it was the dawn of big data analytics, and for Motorola engineers the "big data problem" of the era was Mother's Day. On that single day, millions of people all over the world picked up their phone to call mom. We focused our greatest engineering and analytical energies on how to ensure all of those people got a dial tone and were able to say "I love you."

I wrote the exam in early November 1993 and still remember when the letter from the Illinois Institute of Technology arrived in the second week of December. I was afraid to open it. The result wouldn't affect me going to China, but I was nervous because I'd never failed at any part of my education. Thankfully, the letter said I'd passed.

0 0 0

Before I moved to China, Motorola sent me on a 2.5-day cross-cultural training course in Chicago. I talked to experts and read articles about the psychological impact of living abroad in China and other practicalities, as well as highlights of the almost 5000 years of history that gave rise to modern-day China. I also met a lovely woman named

Betsy who, years later, in 1997, asked me to become one of their experts on doing business in China (that was the official beginning of my firm, Ellis & Associates).

In mid-October, after the training and before I moved to China permanently, Motorola sent me on a "look see" trip. That's when expats see where they'll be working, line up an apartment, and take care of other details. After a 14-hour flight from Chicago to Tokyo, a 4-hour layover, and a 4-hour flight to Beijing, I arrived at around 9:30 p.m. on a cold and foggy Sunday. The airport was in the middle of nowhere, and reminded me of similar facilities in some of the poorest Latin American countries I'd visited. (The airport was rebuilt for the 2008 Olympics, and today it's surrounded by housing estates.) The expressway from the airport into Beijing didn't exist, so my driver, who spoke no English, took a series of bumpy back roads.

Beijing was nothing like it is today. Only four years after Tiananmen Square, China was still in the early stages of making a transition from a rigid Communist regime to introducing private forms of production and Western-style competition to improve the country's economy. (Later, when I moved there, Motorola gave me a fully paid, open-ended, first-class airline ticket with the instructions that if anything like Tiananmen Square happened again, to go straight to the airport and get out.) I also received an additional 25% of my salary as "hardship pay."

There were very few cars in Beijing—most people traveled on foot or by bicycle, although there were buses for longer trips. As foreigners, we initially had to use foreign exchange certificates (FECs), instead of China's currency, the renminbi, and Motorola's travel consultants had warned us to assume all our comings and goings, including our conversations, were being monitored by the Chinese state police. It didn't help that I stood out in China—at well over 6 feet tall, I towered over most locals and had blondish hair and blue eyes. I remember being stared at constantly.

After finding an apartment and getting a car—and all the other things you need to do before moving permanently—I returned to the Beijing airport to make a side trip to Harbin, the capital and largest city of Heilongjiang province in the country's northeastern region, to solve a problem with a switch, which had been offline for a few weeks. I was accompanied by a young Irish-American program manager named Megan Shea, who had studied Chinese in college. She would be my interpreter. Neither the customer nor Motorola's field engineers knew what was wrong.

Like Beijing, Harbin was cold and dreary at that time of year, but it was even more isolated. At the job site, I discovered the problem wasn't the switch but a rat, which had gotten into the switch room, eaten through the plastic wiring, and electrocuted itself. I found the problem in about an hour and solved it within a few hours. The customer was very grateful and wanted to take us to dinner. On our way, Megan warned me that in China it's bad form not to accept whatever hospitality is offered. There were many plates at that dinner, but I especially remember two of them: a whole fish wrapped in a wet towel and baked (when served, the fish was taking its last breaths; apparently, in ancient times, rulers demanded this show to ensure the fish was alive and healthy when cooked) and newly born chicks dipped in chocolate (the chocolate suffocates them; another exceptionally "fresh" dish). Having a lot of international travel and eating under my belt, it still took every fiber of my being to dig into the breathing fish and to bite into a chocolate chick. I can still remember the distinctive sound of the bones breaking in between my teeth as I chewed. The customer and Megan were pleased I had not refused the dishes (though I drank a lot of beer).

Later, while living in China, I ate an amazing amount of exotic food in the name of good manners, including "five snake dishes" (snake blood, intestinal juice, meat, fried skin, and bone broth) as well as fried cockroach and snails. I had to draw the line at monkey brain, an uncommon and exceptionally exotic dish, even in China. When you eat monkey brain, it is usually served on a rotating tray, like a Lazy Susan, that has a hole in the center and a steel band mounted slightly above it. While the monkey is still alive, its head is forced through the hole and held in place by the steel band. The band is tightened until the top of its head is lopped off, with the monkey still writhing. The smell of the brain is one of the most horrible things I've ever experienced. Some kind of grain alcohol is poured into the skull to make a "brain soup." Diners eat it with spoons. Between the visuals and the smell, I had to leave the room. It was the first and only time I refused to eat a dish.

I returned to the U.S., and 2 months later, on January 2, 1994, armed with a completed master's exam but with three classes remaining (and four years in which to complete them), I left again, bound for my two-year assignment in China.

At first I lived in Legend Garden, a newly built expat community that was beautiful but far from the action in the embassy district in downtown Beijing. About a year later, I move into an apartment on the 36th floor of the tallest building in downtown Beijing, which was much better. Despite my facility with languages, I couldn't just "pick up" Chinese. It's a difficult language to learn. I got the hang of about 100 phrases during my time there. Thankfully, a number of Chinese nationals I met spoke English very well, among them Artemis, who worked at Motorola and later became my girlfriend and personal translator. (Artemis wasn't her Chinese name; she chose it as her Western name, although "Artemis" was actually a Greek goddess.)

The Motorola expat team was a very tight-knit group that tended to hang out at Frank's Place, one of a very few Western-style bars in Beijing at that time. Sometimes we mingled with our competitors, like the Swedish firm, Ericsson, and the German firm, Siemens. I remember watching the 1994 Super Bowl at Frank's Place on a signal "stolen" from whatever American station was airing it. That meant we were watching the "house feed," so when the station cut to commercials we could hear the presenters talking among themselves. That was my first experience with the very relaxed attitude toward intellectual property that characterized China and other emerging nations and would later create problems for Motorola.

There was a telecommunications system linking most of the country via landlines, telegraph, radio, and TV, but nothing was as advanced as in Western countries. The landline system, in particular, was considered frustratingly inefficient. The greatest opportunity, it turned out, was in selling cellular infrastructure. By 1993, out of 162 cellular system operators in China, 107 had contracts with Motorola. How important was China to Motorola? The board met in Beijing that year to discuss, among other things, that sales in China promised to outstrip every other emerging market.

The challenge Motorola faced was bringing China up to speed not only in its technological sophistication but also, as an internal Motorola report understated, the "shortage of management talent in the labor supply." The problem, in a nutshell, was that people over the age of 35 had frightening memories of the Cultural Revolution and had learned never to take risks. Those under 35 had been taught that individual ambition was good but improvisation and curiosity suggested that a person was presumptuous and insolent.

Motorola University was the company's education and training arm, associated with the Six Sigma system developed by a Motorola engineer in the mid-80s. (A set of management methods designed to increase quality control, customer satisfaction, and profits, Six Sigma became famous when celebrity CEO Jack Welch, of General Electric, adopted it in 1995 with great success and it became the norm in most corporations.) Most of Motorola's hires in China had undergraduate degrees in engineering and were destined to be middle managers and technologists, since telecom equipment was created by computer-integrated processes. Motorola University provided training for its own Chinese staff as well as the company's joint venture partners, suppliers, customers, and even State government officials, all of whom were taught Western-style organizational structure and business culture.

In part this was a commitment Motorola made to China in exchange for doing business there. But it was also a public relations and brand-building exercise, as well as a long-term solution to the expense of expats. (Compensation and support, not to mention Western-style accommodations, international schools for children, and trips home meant expats cost Motorola about six to ten times that of Chinese managers.)

The biggest part of my job in China was teaching a department of engineers about the switches, base stations, and other products being produced by Motorola and the software that Motorola developed to make it all work. The company was efficient at selling and supporting its products in the field but had no experience in building a development team from the ground up. Throughout this time, I worked closely with Todd Johanson. We were both switch engineers, the guys who wrote the software and built and developed networks with Motorola's switching products.

At a certain point, I realized my training program was not progressing fast enough because we did not have an on-site lab. So I proposed the design and build of a lab to management. They approved and gave me the responsibility to deliver. To build one was, itself, a logistical challenge. First, owing to huge customer demand, every Motorola product was on back order. Moreover, it was both legally complicated and hugely expensive to ship product from the U.S. to China, so many on the U.S. support team were reluctant to do so for an "internal" sale. Also, this was not the just-in-time culture of the U.S. Many of the materials and parts we needed were in short supply, since China was shipping everything it made to the West. (Even though they were stamped "Made in China," it was incredibly hard for me to get my hands on them.) I remember the day came when we moved an EMX5000 into the lab; at the time it was Motorola's biggest cellular switch and a monster. At maximum capacity it had 14 bays, each one 7 feet tall, 19 inches wide, made of solid steel and bolted to the floor with big, thick cables running to it. It was powered by a Power Distribution Frame (PDF), a 1440-kilogram copper container powered by 440 volts, with massive rectifiers that changed the incoming AC current to DC, which the switch electronic boards used. I can still remember the "moving crew" arriving—a team of about 20 Chinese off-duty firemen who carried it up five flights of stairs and into the lab, moving it a few feet at a time, each time grunting *yi, er, san....* ("1, 2, 3" in Chinese).

That lab became the center of everything we did. Every product was made by Motorola, and we could show people how the system worked and how to troubleshoot it as well as test our software. Motorola thought of it as a triumph, and I'd designed it and overseen its construction.

Late in 1995, as my China contract was coming to an end, Motorola hosted an international conference of support personnel in Beijing. I was having a pint with Tadgh O'Reilly, who worked for the company in Ireland. He asked me about my plans after this assignment and I told him I didn't know but really liked living overseas. "Would you consider moving to Ireland?" he asked, explaining that he could see me doing for Ireland what I'd done for China. We put the plans in motion, and on May 1, 1996, I relocated to Ireland and ended up staying there for 3.5 years.

□ □ □

I have fond memories of my time in Ireland, and one of the fondest has nothing to do with Motorola and my work there. Every August, an international competition called the Rose of Tralee is held in the town of Tralee, in County Kerry. The idea is to select one "lovely and fair" Irish rose, based not on appearance, like a beauty pageant, but on personality and suitability to serve as a kind of ambassador for Ireland. The competition is open to both Irish-born young women and women of Irish heritage from around the world, and each one is paired with a young man who serves as an escort.

I applied to be one of the escorts for the 1996 pageant, proving to the committee that I was a well-brought-up, charming, and responsible fellow who would not bring shame to the competition. I became the first non-Irishman to act as a Rose of Tralee escort, paired with the "Limerick Rose," which led to a most unlikely bit of fame: the "Limerick Rose" and I were pictured in the August 1997 issue of *Maxim* magazine.

Work couldn't quite compete with that, but one professional hallmark event was the creation of Motorola's C7 test team. As cellular network technology evolved and improved, we began using better signaling technology to increase reliability, boost *throughput*—the rate of successful message delivery over a communications channel—and provide better data management capabilities. C7 technology, a kind of telephone signaling protocol, was one way to achieve that.

As I mentioned earlier, emerging markets around the world had very poor telecom infrastructure and so mostly leapfrogged from further evolving a landline system to deploying modern cellular technology whenever possible. One thing that most countries learned from their landline days, though, was the importance of *interoperability*, to interchangeably use and accept services from other systems. For a company like Motorola to sell more and more equipment based on the C7 technology, it had to be able to operate with the existing landline equipment.

I was at a meeting in Cork, Ireland, with our leadership team when this business issue was raised. I proposed building a C7 testing team that would travel around the world demonstrating how effectively Motorola's equipment could operate with existing networks. Not only would we highlight our goods and services, but we'd also educate the state-owned telephone companies on how the new technology worked.

Motorola's executives agreed and instructed me to leverage all those hours I'd spent in the lab in Arlington Heights learning how to use test equipment and how to "instrument" a switch. I also used what I'd learned from building a lab and a team in Beijing, and taught the people I'd chosen to join the team to view our work as technical sales.

This project—installing and deploying cellular technology throughout the world, which could be thought of as the foundation of the Internet of Things (IoT)—is the reason I often say that I've been involved in the IoT since 1990.

My assignment in Ireland is significant for another reason: without it, I might not be married to my wonderful wife, Karen.

One customer to which Motorola wanted to sell more equipment was the Peruvian national telecom provider. In February 1998, I was sent to Lima for what was intended to be 2 to 3 weeks of standard testing. It turned out that nothing was standard in Peru and our work took more than 6 weeks to complete. I was supposed to finish up on a Friday and fly back to Cork. But I was scheduled to do some work in Fort Lauderdale, Florida, on the following Monday morning so I suggested that I fly home to Chicago instead, especially since it was the weekend immediately before St. Patrick's Day, which is a big celebration in my hometown. Management agreed, so I boarded a flight to Chicago.

On a cool but sunny Sunday, I went to the South Side Irish Parade with my brothers and sisters. I felt like I'd caught something on the flight back home and was feeling pretty miserable, so as we walked to the rendezvous point where our mother was picking us up after the parade, I said I thought I should go home and sleep. My brother Tom said, "No way. You came all this way to celebrate the holiest of Irish holy days so you're coming with us to Reilly's Daughter."

Located on the corner of 111th and Pulaski, Reilly's Daughter is a favorite hangout among the Irish of the Chicago South Side. I popped a few Advil and agreed to come. At the bar, the first people I ran into were Mr. and Mrs. Daly, who were schoolmates and, later, close friends of my mother. Mrs. Daly, who had also been keeping in touch with me lately as a result of what was then the newfangled AOL email technology, suggested I say hi to her daughter, Karen, who was in another part of the bar.

I'd known Karen since we were toddlers but hadn't seen that much of her since we'd grown up.

Karen and I started chatting at 3 p.m. and didn't stop until she dropped me off at my mom's house close to midnight. I have talked with Karen every day since then. In fact, while I was working in Florida the following 5 weeks, we regularly logged 6-hour phone calls. One weekend we talked for almost 14 hours. (As a Motorola employee, no one can say I wasn't using telecommunications to its maximum potential.) By the end of July 1998, I knew that Karen and I were meant to be together but wasn't sure how to make that happen. I was happy with my Motorola job and was living an expat's life in Ireland while Karen was in Chicago.

As it turned out, Karen had Irish citizenship, a legacy of her grandparents on her dad's side, so I proposed something I hoped she wouldn't refuse: Karen should move to Ireland and stay with me so we could really get to know each other. I told Karen that she and I should date and see how things worked out away from the expectations of family and friends who would be constantly asking how things were going and when we were getting married. (Our parents and their extended gang of close friends thought the idea of a couple of the "kids" getting together was exciting.)

So Karen took a leave from her corporate banking job and moved to Ireland on October 2, 1998. We got engaged the following March, and married in October 2000, with more than 425 people, including 45 friends and relatives from Mexico and Ireland, in attendance.

□ □ □

So what happened to my plan of becoming a priest after I gained some life experience?

Well, in my spare time in China I'd started up a little weekend business taking people to see the Great Wall and camping overnight. I was a big fan of The Grateful Dead and, in August 1994, Jerry Garcia died. A group of us decided we needed to celebrate his life, so early one Saturday morning, eight people in two cars drove to Simatai, a very remote section of the Great Wall of China outside of Beijing. We unpacked our coolers, camp stoves, tents, and batteries (so we could play the Dead's music) and indulged in a bit of everything, from wine and beer to special brownies, and guys and girls paired off.

At about 3 a.m., when everyone was asleep, I suddenly woke up, not sure what had disturbed me. Rather than roll over and go back to sleep, I took my blanket and made my way to a part of the wall, away from my friends, and sat on a ledge. I looked into the darkness, void of human-generated light, lit only by stars. It was a magical, profound moment. I realized why I had awoken so suddenly: I had come to the understanding that I enjoyed my secular and professional life too much. I was never going to become a priest.

What would I tell my devout mom, who thought she was going to have a priest in the family? I didn't go into a lot of detail: "The calling wasn't mine."

4

I'M NOT A CAR GUY, I'M A SOFTWARE GUY

I really loved working at Motorola. I stayed there for almost 21 years, and because of that company I traveled the world and received a generous salary and benefits. I understood the system, and the system was good to me. Much of the time I was overseas, teaching people how our products could work for them, exposing the inefficiencies of products they'd previously been using. I was something like an evangelist for Motorola. I guess that's how I re-directed my interest in the priesthood.

In 2001, Motorola sent me to the University of Notre Dame to an executive MBA program. While there, a professor was concerned by the lack of math skills shown by some of my fellow students. (Surprising because, remember, a lot of the "students" were CEOs and other senior executives at corporations.) I announced that I would do a tutorial for the eight students in my study group. When the day arrived, three-quarters of the class turned up. When the director of the program got wind of that he said, "We'd like to formally hire you for the next academic year." So I designed a multi-module course called Introductory Financial Mathematics, the first class that incoming students took so their math abilities could be assessed and, 6 months later, they returned for a second, more advanced class. Notre Dame kept renewing my contract and, in the end, I taught there for a decade. It was a lot of work, but I must have inherited the teaching gene from my parents because I passionately love educating people.

Teaching fell under the umbrella of my company, Ellis & Associates, which dates back to when I was going to university and still living with my mom. I wanted to receive technical journals for free, and I discovered that a lot of firms would only send them to named companies. So I formed Ellis & Associates, and suddenly technical journals began appearing at my mom's house addressed to John Ellis, Managing Director. (There were, of course, no associates yet.) But it wasn't until years later that I really began using the company. In fact, the same Chicago company (which evolved into Cartus, a global executive relocation business) that had sent me for cross-cultural training before I left for China, later asked me to become one of their "in-the-country" experts on China while I was living in Ireland. My bosses at Motorola gave their blessings so long as it didn't interfere with my time and deliverables. So back then, under Ellis & Associates, I created a training program focused on cultural differences and the impact it had on business. My program was based on the Intercultural Awareness Model (ICAM) developed by Paula Caliqiuri. Using her dimension model, I explained, for instance, the issues an American would have relocating to Mexico for work. Differences like formal versus informal style; group versus individual interests; direct versus indirect communication; and my favorite, controlled versus fluid time. I named the series "How to Do Business Effectively in…" At its peak, I was delivering 20 to 25 sessions a year, covering about two dozen countries. Ellis & Associates had suddenly become an education consultancy specializing in cross-cultural training programs.

By the late 2000s, I knew I'd been at Motorola too long and the company was in trouble. It was a blessing when I was let go in December 2010. I was given a generous package that afforded me a 6-month cushion that allowed me to stay busy with my cross-cultural training programs as well as a few additional contracts that came my way based on my reputation as a software expert.

Then one day I got a tip that there might be an opportunity at Ford.

The Ford team wanted to hire a full-time chief technical officer, but they were balking at what it would cost them to hire someone of caliber. I wasn't that interested in relocating to Dearborn, MI, but it was a requirement of the position. The team soon realized I was the candidate they wanted, but there were some logistical challenges to the paperwork. Having never hired anyone to a senior software position like this, they were struggling to get the appropriate approvals and buy-ins. Rather than risk the deal falling apart, they suggested hiring Ellis & Associates on a 3-month contract to deliver the software strategy for the connected car while they worked at converting the consulting agreement to full-time employment. I was amenable to this approach, although negotiating the contract with Ford's purchasing department in charge of hiring vendors was cumbersome.

I'll never forget the day I received the email stating that everything was in order and that I would be Ford's new global technologist. It was Friday, September 23, 2011, and I was standing in line at the GM-sponsored Test Track at Disney's Epcot Center. The irony.

At the end of that 3-month contract, my full-time employment was ready.

It would be an understatement to say that I'd never imagined working in the automotive industry. To be honest, I didn't give a shit about cars, having never pimped, chipped, or modded any of the ones I'd owned. I had inherited my first car from my dad: a white Ford Taurus four-door sedan. It was hardly a flashy attention-getter in the eyes of most young guys, but it was just transportation to me. Later, a friend of my mom sold me a used midnight-blue Toyota Camry wagon, another sensible, dull family car. I didn't drive much in China, but when I did it was a Jeep Cherokee. In Ireland, I had a right-hand-drive Ford Mondeo, the European version of the Taurus. By the time I was on my way to an interview at Ford in the summer of 2011, I was driving a 10-year-old Toyota Camry XLE sedan. (If none of them would make a hard-core car guy's heart flutter, at least a couple of them were Fords.)

Here's just one way that I was radically different from all the car guys who worked at Ford. At that time and true to this day, if you take two cars in the same class—let's say the Ford Taurus and the Hyundai Sonata—and remove the badges, I find the vehicles basically indistinguishable. If you work at Ford or Hyundai, of course you'll immediately start naming all the subtleties that make them different. I get it, the stitching on the upholstery, the placement of the headlights, the configuration of the trunk, whether they have alloy or steel wheels, what the doors "sound like" when they are closed. But to me, not a car guy, those subtleties were and continue to be lost. Therefore, coming at it from a software perspective, if it's got four wheels and an engine, it's a car.

I had to be careful about saying this kind of stuff when I was speaking publicly, as a representative of Ford, at automotive events. It didn't go over well with hard-core car guys.

But there was a shake-up going on in the industry. When I did my second interview series at Ford, I remember saying that there would be a lot of dramatic technological change coming. Since I'd be the highest-ranked software executive at a traditional car company, I said, "Listen, if I'm doing my job right a lot of people will get pissed off. Therefore, you should fire me if you don't get phone calls on a regular basis from people saying, 'WTF? Fire this Ellis guy.'"

I was hired as Ford's global technologist and immediately began pushing to implement the strategy I'd developed earlier, starting with the Ford third-party software developer program. It took most of 2012 to get the necessary buy-in to make that happen—a first of its kind in the automotive industry and not unlike those at tech companies like Apple, Google, or Facebook. In January 2013, I added "head of developer program" to my title. I was in

charge of integrating mobile technology into our vehicles. Supervising a team of developers, engineers, and marketers, my job was to create the "connected car," striking
the right balance between embedded and off-board technology so drivers could seamlessly extend their mobile
lives into their vehicles.

What does "connected car" mean? Let me illustrate with
a story.

On my first day at the Ford office, I was headed out for
lunch when one of my staff said, "Here, take my car." He
explained that we're all part of the Ford family, that the
insurance is set up to cover all of us, and everyone routinely swaps cars. He gave me his keys, told me where his
Explorer was parked, and suggested a lunch spot. When
I got to his car, it took me a couple of minutes to start it.
(Remember, I drove an 11-year-old Toyota where you put
a key in the ignition and turned it. This was a push-button
start, and I had never before seen one.) Then I thought,
Great, I'll make a Bluetooth wireless connection with my phone
(what's called "pairing"). Let's be clear about this: I build
software. I worked in the cellular industry for more than
20 years. I know all about pairing. But it still took me
10 minutes to do it with this car I'd never used.

What did this tell me? It shouldn't be this hard or take this
long to establish a link to the "connected car" (the whole
basis for Ford's connected car strategy). And yet it did.

So why did it?

First, the process was cumbersome and not at all intuitive. Second, the user manual sucked. Trying to find words like "Bluetooth" or "pairing" was an exercise in frustration. (I later learned that user manuals might as well be called "Cover-Your-Ass Documents." They were mainly designed to satisfy regulators, not be helpful to customers.) Third, for a company that wanted to do "dramatic new things," the products they were working with were seriously messed up.

One question I like to ask people is "When did cars first become connected?" They usually guess the early 90s, or sometime in the 2000s, like 2006 or 2007. It was 1922, when Chevrolet marketed the Chevrolet Radio Sedan, which had huge, heavy batteries under the seats connected to a modified Westinghouse radio and an antennae contraption on the roof. As an option, it cost a third the price of the entire car. It worked, but one radio historian described it as "about as convenient as taking a live orchestra along for a ride." There was so little demand that the company discontinued it, but we can still think of the first car radio as the beginning of the "connected car."

In 1930, brothers Paul and Joseph Galvin, along with William Lear, later an aviation designer, adapted Galvin's "battery eliminator," a device that let battery-operated radios run off a home's 120-volt system, to a Studebaker.

(Remember the origin of the Motorola brand name, "motor" plus "Victrola"?) Prices began dropping after that, and radios became more common in cars. By the late 40s, radios were usually pre-installed, with Motorola producing a third of them.

But the "connected car" of today, at a time when there are more mobile phones than people on the planet, is entirely different. It refers to a vehicle that has internet access and a wireless network. The impact is already being felt—a new car's infotainment system can be synched with our smartphones—and other trends are nearly with us, like cars with sensors that can interact with other cars and objects to improve safety, as well as autonomous (self-driving) cars. All possible because of the miracle of software.

In February 2012, when I stood on a public stage for the first time as a Ford executive, I had prepared a white slide with the Ford logo and my name. That's where the standard presentation fare ended. My message was a little unorthodox: Over an image of a Ford logo, I had written "I'm not a car guy. I'm a software guy and I work at Ford."

That caused quite a commotion. Ford's PR team was up in arms. "Unapproved messaging," they complained. I said, "Folks, celebrate this for what it is. You're now a software company, and you hired a software guy from Motorola." I never knew exactly what happened but someone higher up in the hierarchy must have said "Leave him alone," because from that time on I used it for all of my presentations.

Another question I like to ask is "Who was the first to develop the *modern* connected car?" It wasn't Apple or Google. GM is most often credited with delivering the first connected car, in 1996, with OnStar equipped in the Cadillac DeVille, Seville, and Eldorado. While not the mobile IP (internet protocol) communications we know today, it was an embedded modem that provided very early access to the vehicle.

But it was Ford that first delivered an interactive voice system into a car and, in so doing, enabled connectivity by making it easy to integrate a phone. Initially, Ford was only thinking of safety: "Eyes on the road; hands on the wheel." Little did anyone know that single decision would let Ford take the lead in developing the most connected cars in the world.

In 2007, recognizing that people were bringing their mobile phones into cars anyway, Ford announced a partnership with Microsoft called the Ford SYNC technology. Using applications developed both by Ford and third-party developers, drivers of Ford vehicles—and not just the priciest luxury models—had access to GPS navigation and, with smartphone integration, digital music players, voice-activated phone calls, and audible text messages. One of the marketing lines was "Don't worry, I'm talking to my car." That reminded everyone that people sitting alone in their cars and talking weren't crazy; they were just using the voice-activated function that let them keep their hands on the wheel and their eyes on the road. This technological innovation, originally conceived as a safety feature, let Ford take the lead in having the most connected cars in the world.

In the early days, especially, Ford's developer program was an anomaly. Automakers thought of themselves as mainly in the hardware business: they manufactured cars, minivans, SUVs, and trucks. A year before I joined Ford, technology journalist David Kirkpatrick wrote in *Forbes* that "regardless of industry, your company is now a software company, and pretending that it's not spells serious peril."

I would tell that to the managers and executives at Ford. "Folks, it's the 21st century. You're now in the software business." For the most part, those outside our department looked at me like I was a talented, but eccentric, cousin. *No, no, John, we build cars. We're a hardware company. We're not a software company.*

I guess they hadn't looked too closely at the number of sensors on their own cars. Remember that image I showed in my Zero Dollar Car presentation (see page 7)?

To give you an idea of how far we've come, today's cars have more software (measured as "lines of code"

[LOC]) than the Space Shuttle, which orbited the earth with about 500,000 LOC. The Boeing 777, which entered commercial service in the mid-90s and ironically enough was Alan Mullaly's last plane before becoming CEO at Ford, had approximately 3.5 million LOC. In 2010, the Ford Mustang had around 25 million LOC, and two years later, the Ford Taurus had almost 50 million. During the time I was at Ford, our projection for 2020 vehicles was more than 100 million lines of code.

Many of us know family members or friends who love to tinker with their cars, making various repairs or modifications. Today, though, there's a digital divide. If you know what you're doing, you can still change the oil, air filter, and timing belt, and mess a bit with the tires. But you can't do much else before you have to be in an IT shop doing diagnostics. In fact, automakers are concerned that if amateurs get access to the electronic control units (ECUs) and the software coding that runs them, which operate critical functions, like steering, braking, and throttle inputs, it could affect safety. (Imagine a weekend gearhead tweaking the ECU codes—known as "chipping"—messing up the coding and later the brakes failing, causing a fatal crash.) Small wonder evidence of tinkering can render a warranty null and void.

Despite this, as recently as a few years ago, all of the automakers—except Tesla, of course—were populated with executives who were so far from understanding software that it could be frustrating. Ford's developer program, however, was moving parallel to trends in the industry. A 2016 McKinsey & Co. report, called "Monetizing Car Data: New Service Business Opportunities to Create New Customer Benefits," referred to the challenges facing automakers (also called OEMs, or "original equipment manufacturers"): "High-tech companies, start-ups, alternative mobility operators, data management services, insurers, roadside assistance providers, and infrastructure operators will all be players in the car data monetization landscape. It is the most traditional of automotive players, however, who may find staking a claim most challenging. OEMs and suppliers are accustomed to seven-year product cycles, full control over a stable value chain, consolidated monetization models, and few interactions with end customers."

That's only part of it. Here are a couple of examples. One day I learned that our team was being flagged by quality control for an issue that puzzled me. We'd developed an app that allowed drivers to park their cars and pin the spot on their phones. The GPS on the phone would allow drivers to easily find their car when they returned. (Anyone who's parked in a multi-floor airport garage or outdoors at a huge mall knows this could sometimes come in handy.) But Ford's quality control representative said that the number for the car's GPS and the number for the phone's GPS were different, and that it could cause confusion with the customer.

"But you can't ever make the numbers the same," I explained. "Your smartphone is your phone. The GPS on your phone will always have a different number from the GPS in your car. The point of this feature is to help drivers find their cars, and we've shown that it works. Do you think drivers are going to call Ford to complain that the numbers are different if the feature helps them find their cars?"

"That doesn't matter, John. The numbers are different."

I was stunned. Even if you think people might complain, which I can't believe would happen, you can have a Frequently Asked Questions (FAQ) page and create a YouTube video explaining it. But this rep, who went by the book, thought the answer was not to offer the feature at all to avoid any possible confusion. Or to assign the feature a certain number of "quality issue points" in terms of quality concern. Every car that ships is allowed a certain maximum value of "quality issue points." So long as the total number of points is less than the agreed-to program total, the car is approved to ship. Thus, it was important to me and to our team not to have any "quality issue points." Alas, I lost that argument.

Sometimes things just got comical. In 2012, I was working with a group within Ford called the Battery Electric Vehicle Group that was developing Ford's first all-electric vehicle. A quality control inspector involved in the program had heard that customers would be required to get Ford apps from Apple's app store (as well as Google's store). Like any good quality control person, he said he needed to do a physical inspection of this store, because it's selling a Ford product being used for the vehicle. We had to explain that Apple's app store was not an address on a bricks-and-mortar structure. Later, the same guy wanted a list of all the components of the cloud computing environment because he wanted to verify that waterproof materials were being used. If it was in the cloud, he reasoned, there was condensation and water would be present and, as we all know, water rusts stuff. The team members were giggling about it and stringing the fellow along so I had to explain that the "cloud" is a metaphysical construct, not a water-based entity. It wasn't his fault; he wasn't trained. But it shows how large the gap could be between the software side of the automotive industry and the traditional hardware side.

I'll ask again: Today, can anyone really question whether automakers are, in fact, software companies?

◻ ◻ ◻

In my role as global technologist, it was part of my job to point out—within the company and when I gave talks at conferences and public events—that a new generation of customers today, not to mention our customers of tomorrow, were born with smartphones in their hands. All they've known is a world of digital connectivity. For most of us, our devices are rarely more than an arm's length away and we're not likely to leave home, or get into a vehicle, without them. In the early 20th century, Henry Ford talked about the freedom of the open road; today we want—no, we demand—the freedom of connectivity.

Some of my colleagues in the automotive world didn't believe that consumers would buy a $40,000 car based on whether it works with a $400 device. Which missed the point. The device is nothing more than a physical manifestation of our digital ecosystem choice. We absolutely are concerned with how well a product that we use only an hour or two a day is going to work (or not) with our digital workflows and enabled by the likes of Google and Apple. So, it's the Apple or Android ecosystem that matters, not the 150-gram object with the 5-inch screen. While I didn't have exact data to back me up at the time, later I'd be proven right. A 2015 McKinsey & Co. report, called "Competing for the Connected Customer: Perspectives on the Opportunities Created by Car Connectivity and Automation," stated that "globally, customer demand for car connectivity is increasing at a very high speed: over the past year, the share of customers willing to switch their car brand for better connectivity has almost doubled from 20% in 2014 to 37% in 2015."

Here's another story I love to tell: I have two sets of twins. I remember getting in my wife's car with my then 8-year-old daughters in the back seat (the oldest twins). Her car just has a regular radio in it. When the radio came on the girls heard the tail end of Katy Perry's song "Roar." My daughter, Kate, said, "Daddy, we want to listen to that from the start. Can you hit the back button?"

I said, "I can't do that, Kate. It's a radio."

Her sister, Ciara, said, "Yes, you can, Daddy. We do it all the time. Open Pandora, put in Katy Perry, the channel pops up. The song is 'Roar.'"

"Girls, I'm sorry, but I can't do it. It's a radio. That means there are people out there somewhere who tell you what you can listen to and when you can listen to it."

There was silence for about 30 seconds while the girls processed this information. Then Kate said, "Well, *that's* stupid."

I heard some more whispering, and Ciara said to Kate, "Don't worry, Daddy does software. He can fix it." She was thinking of my car, a Ford, in which I had some experimental software that allowed me to buffer music similar to what a TiVo or DVR does.

Aside from being delighted that my kids have such faith in me, it's important to realize that they are the future car buyers. I've never heard them say "Turn on the radio."

They use Pandora, Spotify, and iTunes, so they say "Can we put on some music?" Why does this matter to automakers? Because 80% of radio listening takes place in vehicles, and people want the same environment that they have on their laptops, tablets, and smartphones to be with them when they're in a vehicle.

I've heard people say "But you can't safely drive a car while texting or using social media." That's true, but consider this: You might think Facebook, for example, is not a form of social media you can use in a car. It's highly interactive, people post things and write comments on it, click on videos, look at pictures. But it's also a communications paradigm that millions of people use to connect with others. So the challenge for automakers was finding a way to integrate Facebook so that Facebook knows you're in a driving mode and adjusts itself. For example, the kind of information that pops up might be an audio message: Someone you know has posted that a group of your friends are going to meet at a certain place and time. That means you can modify your plans and your destination if you want to join them, and you can reply using the microphone. Making that happen is a software issue, one of many that I was interested in while I was at Ford.

When we talk about software on vehicles, we're talking about ECUs, powerful minicomputers in a box, which we also refer to as sensors. They're integrated into three main areas of our cars: power and performance, safety, and entertainment.

Power and Performance

Some of the earliest software used on vehicles is related to performance. In the 1970s and 80s, in response to a growing awareness about air pollution, the federal government introduced regulations controlling emissions. By the early 80s, the only way to effectively reduce emissions with an internal combustion engine was by using a microcomputer that could adjust the spark plug rates and control the fuel mixture and burn rates and other functions. Flash forward to today, and 75 to 100 sensors control virtually every function relating to the car's drivability, such as transmission, steering, and brake performance.

Safety

Software plays a big role in safety. For example, sensors calculate when to apply critical safety features like air bags and anti-lock brakes. Sure, there is a mechanical element to almost everything in a car, but the decision-making process—when to deploy the air bags based on factors like speed and impact or triggering the anti-lock brakes when skidding—is calculated by software.

Entertainment

The car's entertainment capabilities relate to what's called the "head unit." Typically located in the center of the dashboard, what was once simply an AM/FM radio receiver with push buttons is today a complex, integrated electronic system, with a touchscreen and video monitor, encompassing wireless services, MP3 player, GPS navigation, many smartphone apps, and, yes, a radio (AM/FM and satellite).

◻ ◻ ◻

In 2011, with the growing number, and popularity, of apps for smartphones, as well as research showing that one in five respondents acknowledged using apps while driving, Ford realized that the goal wasn't just about managing the use of phones in vehicles, but managing the use of what was on the phones. Their first solution, called AppLink, allowed popular music programs like Pandora and Stitcher to continue to run on a mobile device but gave the driver the ability to fully control them from vehicle controls such as steering wheel buttons, radio knobs, and even voice. A little later I was hired to write that software strategy paper, in which I recommended that Ford make the program open source and develop a corresponding developer program so third-party developers would be encouraged to design apps specifically for use in cars and relieve Ford of having to second-guess which apps consumers might want. I convinced Ford that we needed to make a cash investment, too. Developers building software are mainly interested in volume, and an automaker couldn't deliver. At the time, Ford shipped about 6 million cars a year, and the entire automotive industry shipped about 73 million. But in the mobile world, Samsung, alone, shipped 800 million phones a year.

We supplied developers—starting with a limited number for beta testing and expanding to many—with both a software development kit and a hardware development kit, along with tech support to help them integrate their apps using our SYNC connectivity system and the AppLink application programming interface. We also developed the SmartDeviceLink software that competing automakers could freely use to integrate with their own infotainment platform. The idea was to greatly expand the number, and variety, of apps in the car, making consumers happy, and ensuring that developers' apps would work on as many different manufacturers' cars as possible (rather than have to code their apps differently for many proprietary systems). We were open to pitches from anyone, from the single developer working in a basement to the small boutique outfit to large organizations like Pandora, Major League Baseball, The Wall Street Journal, National Public Radio, and Amazon. So long as it was appropriate to use in a vehicle, we would accept it. Soon we had relationships with 10,000 developers worldwide.

It was a great start. I'd been warning Ford executives that if we didn't find a solution to the smartphone and apps challenge, Silicon Valley would, and pretty soon we won't be building cars, but carcasses, largely controlled by others. The plan had been to avoid letting Apple and Google into the car, to retain control of the vehicle data and prevent these players from becoming even more dominant. But shortly after Ford announced its open-source and third-party developer programs, Apple and Google got in the act, introducing their own smartphone interfaces—CarPlay and Android Auto, respectively. SmartDeviceLink, which was first to the market and taught Apple and Google how to do it, was, for all intents and purposes, a competitor to these two. The problem is that Apple's iOS and Google's Android are the dominant operating systems on almost all cell phones, putting the respective companies in a powerful position with tightly integrated and technically superior solutions.

In the end, Toyota signed on to SmartDeviceLink in January 2016. As of early 2017, Ford and Toyota formed the non-profit SmartDeviceLink Consortium to manage an open-source software platform. As of this writing, others, including PSA Peugeot Citroen, Mazda, Fuji, and Suzuki have joined. Ford ended up supporting both CarPlay and Android Auto, in addition to SmartDeviceLink, although Toyota and a few other automakers still refuse to allow them onto their dashboard, citing security and safety concerns.

0 0 0

In the summer of 2013, Ford's planning department contacted me to say that Larry Page, who co-founded Google along with Sergey Brin and had recently been appointed CEO of the company, was coming to Ford. I was asked to be on the committee preparing for his visit.

"Why is he coming?" I asked.

No one seemed to know.

Later, at the end of a conference call with about 20 people involved in the planning for Page's visit, I was still in the dark. "He's a competitor," I asked. "Can anyone tell me why he's coming?"

Still no response. When I asked again I was kicked off the committee.

That was okay with me. I went back to work. The week of Page's visit, an executive said to me, "Listen, I know we kicked you off the committee—sorry about that—but we need a table of your team's goodies. We've got cars, but you're the only team who's got the kind of cool stuff Larry Page would like."

"Okay," I said. Then I was told a global director, who was a lifetime Ford guy with no background in software, would be doing the presentation. I was asked to meet with him on Wednesday, two days before Page's visit, to brief him on my team's stuff so he could demonstrate it. I wasn't sure how that was going to work out.

On Wednesday, I showed the global director some of the things I'd brought for the demonstration table. I had our TDK, Raspberry Pi, and CAN connectors that let us do cool hacks on a car, as well as the hardware kit from Ford's own open-source hardware program (a precursor to the product that Automatic Labs introduced to much fame and fortune in September 2014). I also had the latest Samsung phone that no one could find anywhere yet and had the Amazon Cloud Player app installed on it, which we'd just signed up to integrate with SYNC AppLink.

"No thanks," he said. "I don't like it. I want Pandora."

I said, "Okay, but do you mind if I ask why?"

"Larry Page won't understand Cloud Player," he said. "So I want Pandora."

I thought I had misheard him. Larry Page, the programmer who invented Google's famous search-ranking algorithm, and CEO of the company? Larry Page *wouldn't understand* Cloud Player?

"With all due respect," I said, "Larry Page will understand Cloud Player, and when we tell him Jeff Bezos authorized it to be used on our system, he'll know that Bezos knows all about Ford's program and is involved. Trust me, the messaging, both direct and indirect, is all about this."

"No," he said. "I want Pandora."

The next day I had meetings in downtown Detroit, and that night went out for drinks with some friends. We had a little too much fun and I didn't bother checking my emails. The next morning, I arrived to set up our stuff on the demonstration table wearing jeans and a button-down jean shirt.

One of my colleagues, who was also setting up a table, said, "It's great that you're presenting today."

"No," I explained, "I'm just in the background. The global director is presenting."

He raised his eyebrows. "Have you checked your email?"

He was right. Someone higher up the ladder had decided that I should replace the global director as the presenter.

"Hey, John," one of the executives said. "This is shirt-and-tie, like an executive meeting."

I said, "Larry Page is coming. This isn't a shirt-and-tie meeting."

Page arrived dressed in standard Silicon Valley attire: black Converse trainers, black jeans, a t-shirt, and a cotton sports jacket. When the time came, I stood up and said, "Larry, I don't expect you remember me, but I was part of Motorola's engineering team that brought out the first Android device."

Page said, "Yeah, I remember. Your team solved the Linux power problem."

"Yes," I said.

"Thank you," said Page. "It was a great product."

All around me, the Ford gang were exchanging amazed glances, as if to say, *WTF, Larry Page knows Ellis?*

I was supposed to do a 10-minute presentation, but Page continued to ask me questions for at least another 5 minutes. I told him all about Ford's connected car strategy and how the company wanted to win. Moreover, I showed him how Ford wanted to use all the standard approaches that a company like Google would use (open source, third-party developer programs, APIs, etc.).

"This is really amazing," said Page. "How can I help?"

"Well," I said, "funny you should ask that question..."

I explained that I was working with Patrick Brady, Android's director of engineering, and needed more time with him because I feared a lot of what's happening with Android would happen in the auto sector, too. I wanted Google to make some fundamental changes in Android to better support SmartDeviceLink. "I really want to get in front of that."

"Okay," said Page. "I'll make sure that happens."

Ford's COO at the time, Mark Fields, had been at the event and later he introduced himself. "I've heard many people tell me our strategy around software and cars," he said. "Until today I was confused, but now I'm starting to understand it. I need to spend more time with you."

So for the next 4 months, I went to Mark's office and spent anywhere from 60 to 90 minutes each visit talking to him about our connected car strategy. Although I hadn't come up with the Zero Dollar Car concept yet, that's more or less what I outlined: how the connected car ties into big data, and how this phenomenon was going to transform the world. How most people are alone in their cars and, in the U.S., they drive an average of 75 minutes a day "with intent and purpose"—that is, to get from Point A to Point B (unlike decades ago, when people might have gone for a Sunday drive with no particular destination in mind). How with the connected car and its myriad sensors, it's possible to identify a driver's gender, ethnography, demographic, and even compile data on traveling patterns. I told him what an extremely valuable, captive audience there was, and that we at Ford had to get in front of it.

I showed Mark a sample word cloud illustrating why Google and all the other tech firms were so interested in the connected car. It showed a sample of words spoken in select Ford vehicles over a number of months (with consent of their owners). There were two dimensions of measurement. The first was the frequency of the word spoken in the vehicle cabin (the bigger the word, the more frequent its occurrence). The second was the accuracy of the word. Most voice recognition systems utilize a Bayesian tree approach to determine "what" the word is that was spoken (basically a scientific guess). In our diagram, the darker the green, the more accurate the prediction of the word. The word "restaurant" showed prominently in dark green and was the largest word on the graph. I said to Mark, if a driver in a Lincoln SUV was interested in finding a restaurant and asked his on-board system for help, an upscale restaurant chain like Capital Grille would pay a fistful of money for access to that potential customer to influence their decision on where to go for a meal. And for the same word, but spoken in a Ford Focus, a restaurant like Outback Steak House would pay slightly less money for access to that potential customer. That's value, and Ford could make money from it. We could sell the data to Google.

Unfortunately, my team and I were never able to find traction within the company to pursue the idea.

Toward the end of our 4 months, I told Mark that I knew he was looking to hire a connected car business leader and that I wanted to put my name in the mix. He asked how I knew he was planning to hire someone. I knew because internal executives applying for new positions at Ford require a "book"—a detailed explanation for why they're suited for the job. Two long-term Ford executives were applying for the connected car leadership role, and they'd all come to me over the last few months for help writing their "book," since I knew more than anyone did about the connected car.

In the end, Mark hired a senior marketing guy from GM, although at least he sent me a nice note apologizing and explaining they decided to go in a different direction. That was January 2014. By October of that same year, the new executive director, connected vehicle and services, had few staff or resources, which was frustrating to me because my team would be implementing the plans. It became apparent to me that Ford was not really committed to a connected car strategy, at least at that time. It was no secret I was out of sorts. Finally, on October 30 at 5:00 p.m., I was given a package and my tenure at Ford was over.

5

THE SOURCE
IS WITH YOU

Google has shown us that any software company—
Facebook, Apple, Microsoft—could partner with one
of the "tier one" companies that are direct suppliers to the
automotive manufacturers to build a car. That's also where
the Zero Dollar Car construct comes into play. Software
companies have reinvented the traditional business paradigm. Look at Google, for example. It gives us both email
addresses and the capacity to search the internet for free.
Except it's never "free." We don't pay money for it, but
we do give Google all of our valuable personal data in
exchange for email and search.

With cars, what had once been a pricey piece of inert hardware that took us from point A to point B is now imbued with life: It constantly generates data. This represents a profoundly different way of thinking about business, and everything can be traced back to what I've been dealing with since my days at Motorola: open source software.

What is it? In the 1960s and 70s, most software was created in labs—both within academe and in progressive corporate R&D departments—by engineers and scientists who believed in sharing their knowledge and learning from each other. As technology evolved and the use of computers grew, software became more proprietary. Today, if software is open source, the source code is available, although there can be limitations—for example, licenses, non-disclosure agreements, the ability to view the code only on the software owner's system. But a lot of open source software is available on the internet for anyone to read, customize, and distribute, and it usually just comes with some kind of license that acknowledges the rights of the original creator. There are two big advantages of open source: it encourages creativity, since developers tend to work on projects that really inspire them unconstrained by corporate protocols, and the many eyes examining the software increase the likelihood of spotting bugs in the system.

Many see Richard Stallman as the father of open source, although he later rejected the term, arguing that its associations were too linked to business interests. Stallman, an idealist, was part of the early hacker culture of the mid- to late 70s, when software was routinely shared, even by manufacturers, and everyone learned from everyone else. But by the 80s, creators of software were increasingly using copyright to retain control of the source code, making it proprietary and preventing cooperative sharing. To work, open source software should be free, although not "free" in the sense of "free beer" but "free" in the sense of "freedom" and "liberty." As a developer, for example, I've always believed that I should be able to study software I'm going to use and be able to modify it, and, if I do, circulate those modifications back to the community.

In 1984, Stallman founded the GNU Project with the goal of creating a free operating system based on AT&T's established and stable, but proprietary, Unix system. (GNU stood for "GNU's Not Unix.") Less than a decade later, under a licensing regime called the GNU General Public License, a Finnish programmer named Linus Torvalds launched the initial release of what today we call Linux, a Unix-like operating system that worked on Intel-based computers. (Today, Google's Android, based on the Linux system, dominates the smartphone and tablet markets, and Linux is also the leading system used on servers and big, mainframe supercomputers.)

Meanwhile, in the mid-80s, Apple's Steve Jobs understood that software would sell hardware and that he needed to convince people to build software for the Mac. One of his most brilliant hires was a marketing professional named Guy Kawasaki, who became one of the first of what's known as "software evangelists"—essentially salesmen and promoters who inspire software developers to create applications that can be used on their tech company's products. At that time, developers were part of a tiny niche industry; today, according to Evans Data Corp.'s 2016 Global Developer Population and Demographic Study, there are more than 21 million software developers around the world, a number that will increase to 25 million by 2025. They are the heart of a mobile app industry, representing $25 billion U.S. in direct and indirect revenues.

Do you remember Netscape? I imagine anyone over the age of 40 would. Created by Marc Andreessen (an evolution of his earlier Mosaic browser), it was the first really usable browser that had graphic capabilities, and it became the dominant way for people to "surf the web" in the 1990s. That's what made Microsoft's Bill Gates, who had been slow to embrace the internet, wake up and develop Internet Explorer. The radical key to this technological development was open source.

In 1997, Eric Raymond, a software developer, wrote an essay called *The Cathedral and the Bazaar: Musing on Linux and Open Source by an Accidental Revolutionary*. The "cathedral" is hierarchically structured, a closed corporate model. Access to software code is restricted to a small, carefully selected group. The "bazaar" is open, loosely structured, milling with people. In this model, code is developed over the internet, publicly available to many who can study and experiment with it, but Raymond acknowledged that "open" wasn't the same as "free," which made his theories more attractive to business. It was a manifesto to take open source into the future.

At Netscape Communications, this became a source of existential angst. Wouldn't opening up proprietary information to anyone be giving away shares, risking the entire structure of a corporation? Andreessen embraced that risk and the rest is history. He became the first to turn a cathedral into a bazaar. (Today, Andreessen is a billionaire, and Netscape later evolved into today's Mozilla Firefox browser.)

I became involved in open source while I was at Motorola, and was part of the group that transferred the idea of a software developer team, well-established in the desktop computing world, to the world of mobile devices. Do you remember when I earlier mentioned the first commercially available cell phone? Known as "The Brick" because it was about the size and weight of one, the Motorola DynaTAC 8000X went on the market in the early 80s, cost more than $3000, gave you 30 minutes of use on its battery, and allowed you to do nothing but make phone calls and store numbers in a simple contacts folder. As cell phones improved, more apps became available, but whether you bought a phone from Motorola, Nokia, Samsung, or any other company, what was available on your phone was what the company provided—typically things like calendars, calculators, and ring tones. In a fiercely competitive environment, manufacturers protected trade secrets and developed apps themselves—the "cathedral" model. There was no appetite for allowing independent developers access to what was seen as proprietary code that formed the foundation of your product and, therefore, there existed no vast menu of apps that you, the consumer, could download to personalize your device.

But as the internet grew, customers wanted on their phones what they could access on their home computers. When the earliest games were introduced on phones, people began to see the device as something more than a tool on which to make phone calls. An early solution was created by a consortium that included Motorola, Nokia, and Ericsson: Wireless Application Protocol (WAP), which allowed cell phones to offer many of the advantages of the internet, including email and online services like news, weather, and stock prices. But soon enough companies began building more sophisticated mobile platforms that became the building blocks for today's smartphones. (RIM

BlackBerry was among the first. Motorola partnered with Samsung, Nokia, and Ericsson to create the open source Symbian Foundation based on the Symbian OS. By the late 2000s, Apple's iPhone iOS and Google's Android were also on the market.)

Once we had smartphones that could take apps, the open source developer industry could take off, but it took another circumstance to make that happen. In the late 90s, there were a number of integrated development environments (IDEs), and many companies made money selling and supporting these programming tools. Thinking of Raymond's *The Cathedral and the Bazaar*, people at IBM began asking themselves, *Is there really any money to be made in the tooling side of the business? What if we were to give away our tools? Would more people build apps for our products?* In 1998, IBM began developing an applications platform that would be named Eclipse, and in 2001 they decided to embrace the open source licensing and operating model to attract the largest number of developers to participate. Along with eight other organizations, IBM established the Eclipse Consortium and, later, released it from its corporate moorings and established the not-for-profit Eclipse Foundation, an open source ecosystem dedicated to developing software for Java applications as well as other programming languages.

I was at Motorola during this period, part of the team that created the first third-party software program for mobile devices using open source software. But Motorola didn't fully understand the concept. It's "open," yes, and it's "free," but open source still has licensing responsibilities, terms, contracts. Years later, the company ran into a big problem with an early touch screen-equipped flip phone called the Ming. It was selling millions of units in Asia, so Motorola wanted to introduce it to the U.S. There was a problem, though: All of the software on the Ming was open source, and the team in China building the product were lax about documenting copyright. Some of the software was being presented as Motorola's when it was in fact built by third-party developers. The company's legal department advised that although it would be counter to Motorola's policies, the Ming could probably be distributed in Asia, which didn't have nearly the robust copyright protection of North America and where there would be little likelihood of a lawsuit, but nowhere else.

Then we were served with a legal notice by a Berlin-based programmer named Harald Welte. I looked into who he was and learned that Welte, a firm believer in copyright, ran a site called GPL Violations, referring to the open source-based GNU Public License. He had purchased a Ming to study what software was on it and discovered that Motorola wasn't following all the GPL licensing requirements. I advised Motorola that he wasn't in it for the money so he never settles. He wants companies to restructure and fix the problems that led to copyright infringement. So Motorola paid a small penalty, and to their credit, fully embraced the organizational structure changes needed to fully work with open source software. An example of such a change was supporting me and a few others as we helped establish the company's Open Source Review Board to ensure that we established the provenance of all software being used in our products.

Both at Motorola and, later, at Ford, I became an evangelist myself, talking about the advantages and ethical responsibilities of the open source construct as a business practice and proposing ways to build fiduciary inputs to make it happen. In my role running Ford's developer program, I repeated over and over that automakers had to see themselves as software companies.

Even today, the executives running the traditional auto sector are struggling to come to terms with this reality. When I was at Ford, it was like swimming upstream trying to convince executives who thought of themselves as hardware manufacturers to see themselves as running software companies. (Motorola never made that leap and ended up losing money and share value before splitting into two divisions, one of which was acquired by Google in 2012 and sold to Lenovo Group Ltd. two years later.)

Ford has been similarly slow to make the transition, although that was true of every traditional automaker.

Historically, automakers saw the vehicles they built as hardware and only built into that hardware features that were going to be used at that time on that model. The average consumer could add a few high-performance modifications, like different tires, if they wanted to, and a minority of "modders" (people who could modify stuff) could "break" their engines to push the performance barriers. (This has become harder and harder in an age where tinkering with a car requires access to source code and high-tech diagnostic tools.) For the most part, when new innovations were invented by automakers, they were features on the latest model, and customers who wanted them would have to buy a new car.

Did that change? A bit. When I was at Ford I took what I'd learned about open source and our team created the technology that allowed people to connect their smart-phone to their car. Originally called AppLink and later SmartDeviceLink, with this technology, Ford had the opportunity to do things it had never been able to do before. For example, consider a vehicle manufactured in 2010 but designed in 2007. At the time of design, there was very limited streaming music and Spotify had not yet been created. And yet, by 2015, people were immersed in all sorts of streaming music services like Spotify and Pandora. Using the AppLink technology, we were able to deliver Spotify and Pandora to those consumers who had purchased certain 2010 Ford vehicles. Talk about delighting your customers. And yet, there were many within the company who couldn't understand why we would invest in such technology and enable such an offering. They reckoned that if the customer wanted streaming, they should purchase the newer vehicles that supported it—a classic hardware vendor view where you only make money on the sale of the hardware.

It's the difference between what I call a "ship-and-forget" company and a "ship-and-remember" company. Traditional automakers, for example, like most hardware companies, have little or no contact with end users after a sale is made. In fact, if you have to think about a product after it's on the market, it's probably because of some bad news, like a serious safety issue prompting a recall.

In today's world of connectivity, where there's software that can be upgraded after a sale, or new features that can be added via remote software updates, companies have to embrace "ship-and-remember." That means continuing to engage with customers long after the product is shipped. No company better symbolizes this today than Tesla.

Tesla first did things differently because, from the beginning, CEO Elon Musk didn't see his company primarily as an automaker even though he made cars. He has described Tesla as a "Silicon Valley software company" and also said that he designed the Model S to be a very sophisticated "computer-on-wheels" that could be updated the same way we update phones and laptops.

Open source was a key factor in this. Although Tesla began with a wall covered in patents at its head office—out of concern that big automakers would copy its technology, flood the market with electric cars, and use their size to unfairly compete—it later adopted an open source policy. Aside from Musk's stated claim that this would help foster a faster-growing electric car industry, he no doubt also noticed that his fears about the big automakers were baseless: They were all very slow to make the shift to vehicles that didn't burn hydrocarbons and even slower to fully embrace and understand the power of software in terms of product differentiation and customer satisfaction.

This was even true of connectivity. Where I tried, with mixed results, to make Ford's vehicles truly connected, Musk accomplished it with his electric cars. With its ability to update software and patch vehicles remotely, Tesla can add new features as well as resolve problems—including safety issues that would involve a recall with any other car—almost instantly, and this capability also addresses the problem of quickly responding to a truly 21st century issue: hacking threats.

In the winter of 2015, Tesla announced software updates to the popular Model S that introduced an early, semi-autonomous version of what may become a fully functioning autopilot system, as well as a feature that provides automatic braking when the vehicle senses a potential collision. While some of the luxury car brands offer these features, they were installed on the vehicle before a customer bought it. Only Tesla remotely updates its software to add new features *after* a car has been purchased.

Let me explain why this is revolutionary. Tesla didn't have to install new hardware to upgrade its vehicles with autopilot. When customers bought their Model S, the sensors that would allow for autopilot when that feature was ready were already installed. At that time, Tesla owners could decide to buy the new function and, if they wanted it, Tesla could do an over-the-air update. Overnight the car you bought without semi-autonomous autopilot suddenly had it. This ties into the way customers who bought the Model S were offered a cheaper 60-kilowatt hour battery pack version or the 75-kilowatt hour version, which offered greater acceleration and range. (Tesla has since discontinued the 60-kilowatt option.) If those who were driving the 60-kilowatt hour battery pack wanted to upgrade, they didn't have to take their car into a dealership to have new hardware installed. All they had to do was notify Tesla they wanted to upgrade and engineers "unlocked" (via a software update) the additional 20% of the battery's capacity.

Tesla builds into its cars the potential to add premium performance features (battery capacity) or new technology when it's developed (semi-autonomous autopilot). Both value and functionality can be added in the future, and with each software update, Tesla turns customers into fanatics of the brand. The car is not a static asset but a delivery mechanism for the highly dynamic and evolving software that provides customer delight. Moreover, Tesla now has the flexibility to decide if they want to give the software for free to the customer or charge them (as in the case of the Autopilot mode, which when it was first released cost $3000 U.S. for existing Model S owners to activate in their vehicles). Since the Model S was first released in September 2012, Tesla has done more than 30 software updates that have increased the value of the vehicle. For update 8.0 in 2016, Tesla added a "cabin overheat protection" feature. If the Tesla vehicle detects occupants (child or pet) in the locked vehicle, and the temperature hits a certain threshold, it automatically turns on the air conditioning and circulating air to maintain a survivable in-cabin temperature and thereby avoid the terrible tragedy of people or animals dying because of heat while being locked in a vehicle. This was done purely via software, as all the hardware, developed for other purposes, was already in the vehicle. Those readers who have experience in the traditional automotive sector know that such a feature, while technically possible in other automaker's electric vehicles, would only ever happen after an arduous business case review. Only then would they develop detailed specifications and request quotes from tier-one companies like Bosch or Continental for the work so that the feature could be rolled out, years later, in new cars only.

All this raises many complicated and intriguing questions about automobile ownership. Let's consider one: insurance. Its foundation has been based on a static asset—a piece of hardware called a car or truck—to which it applied actuary tables to calculate coverage based on the expected capability and use of that asset. But what happens if the Tesla Model S purchased last month gets a software update and now goes faster and further, or has an autopilot function that wasn't there when the insurance was purchased? Or has a cool new in-cabin temperature feature designed to save lives? It's now a different car. What is insurance in a world where the underlying asset could change from week to week, month to month? For that matter, what happens to ownership itself when the data being produced by a product is more valuable than the product itself? Do you even own your car, in the traditional sense, when so much of a vehicle's value is in its software? Could automakers claim your right to resell no longer applies because you're just licensing the software?

That's what makes Tesla so profound a disrupter in the automotive sector. The traditional automakers who look at

Tesla and think the threat is from its fancy electric cars are missing the point. The traditional automakers are facing a huge and radical threat because the business model on which their industry rests is coming apart. In a sense, it's a bit like Airbnb, which is upending the hotel industry even though it owns no hotel rooms, or Uber, which is upturning taxi companies and their fleets of cars even though Uber itself owns no cars.

Traditional companies facing that kind of competition can't do things the old, established way. In the case of automakers, those that can't make the shift from "ship-and-forget" to "ship-and-remember" are unlikely to be in business for much longer.

There is no better example of that than the news in 2017 that Tesla surpassed both GM and Ford to became the most valuable car company in the U.S. (As of this writing, Tesla's stock was valued at $51.54 billion, compared to $50 billion for GM and $45 billion for Ford.) How is that possible when GM sold 10 million cars in 2016, and Ford sold 6.6 million, dwarfing Tesla's 76,230 vehicles shipped? And how is it possible when both GM and Ford were profitable, whereas the luxury electric vehicle maker lost $675 million?

There are several reasons. Everyone agrees that electric cars represent the future, but despite GM's Bolt and Ford's all-electric Focus, Tesla is seen as being by far the industry

leader in electric vehicles. The company's battery technology is more advanced than anyone else's, and it now
has the Gigafactory, a facility in Nevada that will be able
to meet Tesla's need for vast quantities of batteries. Tesla
has built an impressive sales network, and the quality of
the cars themselves, with their emphasis on ever-evolving
software, is high. Then there's the less tangible factor: If
Elon Musk's SpaceX can successfully put a rocket into space
and bring it back to Earth, surely that kind of innovation
will benefit its cars as well. Musk himself is a Silicon Valley
darling. But more than anything else, the real value of
Tesla is that the company writes the majority of software
that is on its vehicles. This is in comparison to traditional
automakers, who write very little of their own software.
And what they do write is generally limited to the engine
control. Because of that one difference, Tesla is seen as a
company that can make changes quickly, introduce new
features on existing vehicles, and continually delight their
customers. Add to that a skepticism about whether the big
automakers are nimble enough to pivot and adapt. Can we
really be all that surprised that the investment community
thinks Tesla is a good bet?

The Tesla effect goes beyond the auto industry. Another
example of a transportation-related organization facing
challenges is the American Automobile Association (AAA,
pronounced "Triple-A"), a venerable non-profit that's been

around since 1902. It offers emergency roadside assistance, maps, and trip planning, travel bookings, insurance, member discounts, and other services. I've been doing some consulting with the AAA, and at one point I posed a rhetorical question: Why didn't you folks create Uber? You have nearly 56 million members, all of whom own cars. Yet it took a couple of imaginative kids to figure out that all you had to do to form a successful service company and shake up an entire sector was create technology that could connect people who had a vehicle with people who needed a ride. The AAA had an existing infrastructure, a capitalized company, insurance, and access to drivers. All it lacked was the technology … and the original idea.

Of course, the technology is arguably the hardest part. Nonetheless, let's look at this technology company called Uber. How hard would it be for them to create an insurance service, offer roadside assistance, provide discounts? Why couldn't Uber become an association that would replace AAA? What I was trying to illustrate is that Uber is a potential disrupter. But not just Uber, any such software technology company. Because once the technology problem is solved, and you can harness the flood of data and commercialize it, the barrier to entry into any industry or into any company isn't high.

This brings us back to the Zero Dollar Car concept and how the radical evolution of big data is poised to change almost everything in our lives. It's not restricted to our vehicles, either, although that may be the origin story. With the irresistible urge to stick a sensor in almost any product, the line has blurred between hardware and software, and David Kirpatrick's claim that every company is a software company becomes even more applicable. Increasingly it involves virtually everything we buy, from homes to appliances to baby products to, yes, even sex toys.

6

THE INTERNET OF SO MANY THINGS

A connected sex toy? Does anything better illustrate just how pervasive the Internet of Things (IoT) has become? An Ottawa-based company, Standard Innovation (U.S.) Corp., markets the We-Vibe, a vibrator remotely controlled via a Bluetooth connection after customers download the We-Connect app on their smartphone. The app's "connect lover" feature, which the company promised was a secure connection, let remote partners exchange texts and video chats and control a paired We-Vibe device.

Figure 6 *I'm Not a Thing Guy; I'm a Software Guy*

In 2016, a woman in Chicago filed a class-action lawsuit in an Illinois court—she's identified only as N.P., given the intimate nature of her circumstances—stating that only after she had bought the $130 U.S. device and used it on several occasions did she learn that We-Connect recorded her usage: the date, time, and duration it was in use; the settings she used; and the temperature of the vibrator. What's more, the data and the user's email address were sent to the company's servers in Canada. According to the suit, she "would never have purchased a We-Vibe had she known that in order to use its full functionality, [Standard Innovation] would monitor, collect, and transmit her usage information through We-Connect."

While there was no hack involved, and there seems to have been no evidence that Standard Innovation used the information for anything other than research to tweak the product, the company filed a settlement in March 2017 to pay nearly $4 million U.S. to resolve the privacy claims.

Talk about bad vibes!

But this litigation illustrates the kinds of issues raised by the IoT as more and more devices of every kind are equipped with sensors that can capture, store, and transmit data. It may have begun with the connected car, but now almost anything can be connected.

According to a 2016 Cisco report, annual global Internet Protocol (IP) traffic is at or beyond the zettabyte threshold (one sextillion bytes) and is expected to reach 2.3 zetta-bytes by 2020, the same year it is predicted that more than 1.4 billion smartphones will be shipped—each one carrying sensors that can collect all kinds of data. And smartphone use is expected to exceed PC traffic. A zetta-byte is too large for most of us to imagine. Measured in bytes, tack on 21 zeroes, or think of a zettabyte as approx-imately fitting on 75 billion 16-gig iPads.

That's an exponential leap in the amount of data being produced, and the IoT is the biggest contributor. The IoT refers to countless everyday objects equipped with sensors that can record and report data, everything from microwaves, light bulbs, running shoes, toothbrushes, baby monitors, and pacemakers to bridges, farming equipment, and aircraft jet engines.

When I was putting together my IoT World keynote presentation in May 2016, I asked my daughter, Kate, what a "thing" was. That prompted us to start counting "things" in our house: water tank, faucets, doors, refrigerator, freezer... We stopped after getting to a thousand, but there were certainly more "things" than that.

Then I went to see the city manager of our village and asked how many "things" were in the village. We started counting trees, pipes, intersections, buildings... We stopped when we got to a million, even though there were more things that that.

To actually do the calculation, I went to the U.S. Census Bureau to find out how many cities there are in the U.S. as of May 2016. The number is 35,000 cities of various sizes. Then I checked on how many houses, condos, and apartments there are in the U.S. There are 124.6 million. When you work the math on the number of things in a house and the number of houses, plus the number of things in a city and the number of cities, you end up with nearly 160 billion. And that's in the U.S. alone.

The question I often ask is "How many of our public officials, let alone homeowners, know about software, and know that any product they buy that is powered by software not only should be updated, it *must* be updated?" In my experience, very few.

Toy manufacturers are creating microphone-enabled toys that children can talk to and the toy responds. Is it surprising that parents are beginning to ask "Where are my kids' words going and what are you doing with them? Even if it's turned off, how do I know it's not listening?"

Another voice-activated device is Alexa, the name given to Amazon's Echo, a voice-controlled personal assistant. It's a black cylinder, about the diameter of a soda can and standing 10 inches high, equipped with 7 microphones and connected, through Wi-Fi, to the cloud. When you trigger it by saying its name, "Alexa," it "wakes up" and will answer questions. (It can also be programmed to "wake up" to the words "Amazon" or "Echo," or turned on using a hand-held remote.) When asked a question, Alexa sends the data to Amazon's servers and instantly provides an answer. Later, by looking at Amazon's smartphone app, you can delete the audio files. Alexa stores 60 seconds' worth of audio in its memory, which is what lets it instantly respond when it hears its name, but, according to Amazon, those 60 seconds are stored locally in the device, not transmitted to the cloud, and they're erased each time the device is used. So while Alexa is always "listening"—ready to respond to its name—it isn't always recording and transmitting data. You can also manually turn off the microphones.

Is there any chance those microphones could be hacked, allowing someone to eavesdrop on the conversations and activities around your home? Amazon insists it couldn't happen, but there is a saying popular in cyber security circles: Anything that can be connected will be connected; and anything that is connected is capable, sooner or later, of being hacked. (For example, in March 2017 WikiLeaks released "Vault 7," a collection of CIA files that detailed how the spy agency worked on hacks that would turn Android and iOS devices, PCs, and Samsung smart TVs into potential listening devices.)

Some of the most dramatic hacks have been directed toward the most connected of all things: automobiles. In 2015, Chris Valasek and Charlie Miller, a pair of "white hat" researchers—"white hat" refers to ethical computer security experts who test information systems, as opposed to malicious "black hat" hackers out to profit from their actions or create damage—remotely hacked a Chrysler Jeep Cherokee being driven on I-64 near St. Louis by Andy Greenberg, a *Wired* journalist. Greenberg's description of what happened tells it best:

As the two hackers remotely toyed with the air conditioning, radio, and windshield wipers, I mentally congratulated myself on my courage under pressure. That's when they cut the transmission.

Immediately, my accelerator stopped working. As I frantically pressed the pedal and watched the RPMs climb, the Jeep lost half its speed, then slowed to a crawl. This occurred just as I reached a long overpass, with no shoulder to offer an escape. The experiment had ceased to be fun.

At that point, the interstate began to slope upward, so the Jeep lost more momentum and barely crept forward. Cars lined up behind my bumper before passing me, honking. I could see an 18-wheeler approaching in my rearview mirror. I hoped its driver could see me, too, and could tell I was paralyzed on the highway.

"You're doomed!" Valasek shouted, but I couldn't make out his heckling over the blast of the radio, now pumping Kanye West. The semi loomed in the mirror, bearing down on my immobilized Jeep...

Unlike evil hackers bent on creating mayhem or worse, Valasek and Miller revealed all the details of their hack to Chrysler so the company could release a patch before they publicly reported on their exploits at the 2015 Black Hat security conference in Las Vegas, where thousands of hackers from more than 100 countries meet to discuss the cyber security issues of the future. What most do not know or realize is that immediately after the Valasek and Miller presentation, on the same stage, another set of hackers presented a similar hack against the Tesla Model S. Why didn't it receive the same press coverage as the Chrysler hack? Because the vulnerability had been patched over-the-air about 3 months previously and there was no longer an issue. And thus, no story. Which sadly, was the story. That Tesla had built a product to "do it the right way" was not commented on by the press.

Even more disturbing, the issue isn't restricted to consumer automobiles. In 2016, a group of cyber security researchers from the University of Michigan sent digital signals through the internal network of a big rig truck, allowing them to control acceleration, interfere with the semi's braking systems, and tinker with readings on the vehicle's instrument panel. One revelation was that the attack was made easier because most industrial vehicles use a common network communication standard. Another was that no password was required to log in. Considering the size of industrial vehicles and the fact that many carry hazardous cargo—not to mention the memory of recent terrorist attacks in France, Germany, and Sweden where industrial vehicles were used as weapons—this is a huge concern. The vulnerability of industrial vehicles doesn't only include tractor-trailers, garbage trucks, cement mixers, school buses, and agricultural equipment. It also involves the military.

I've given talks to the U.S. military on vehicle hacking during which I ask, "What do heavy trucks, buses, and construction vehicles all have in common with your vehicles?" The answer: They all use Caterpillar engines and Allison transmissions because the U.S. military requires all vehicle parts be sourced from U.S. companies. I tell them about the big rig hack, and then ask them to imagine a 20-year-old U.S. Army driver specialist whose vehicle is remotely hacked and has his vehicle remotely stopped during a mission. That young man becomes a target. What if he's the lead driver and has now stopped an entire convoy on a road in Afghanistan or Iraq? What if hackers start sounding the horn when the vehicle should be running silent, or turn on the lights when it should be running dark? This is a good argument for why the military should instruct vendors on what software to supply as well as what specific sensors and configurations are required for all of its vehicles.

But hacking isn't the only issue. There are also privacy concerns.

In 2015, after a man was killed in a hot tub at the home of James Andrew Bates of Bentonville, Arkansas, investigators noticed that Bates owned several "smart" devices, including a Nest thermostat, a Honeywell alarm system, a wireless weather monitoring system, and an Amazon Echo. Since Bates was a suspect, they seized the Echo and requested from Amazon the voice recordings, presumably hoping the data would provide some useful evidence to help them identify the killer. Aside from Bates or others in the home using Alexa in the conventional way, the device can also be activated if it hears a word that sounds similar to "Alexa," or if the word "Alexa" is said by someone on a TV or radio broadcast. In theory, that might have happened just in time to capture some key evidence.

We all know that police routinely seize home computers, cell phones, and other personal electronics during investigations, but this case presented a different scenario: Do people have a reasonable expectation of privacy from their voice-activated "smart-home" personal assistants, like Amazon Echo or its competitor, Google Home, which are thought to be "always listening"? At first Amazon refused to comply with the police warrant, which might have led to legal action and a precedent set, but the issue was resolved when Bates granted Amazon permission to provide his data to authorities.

It certainly raises the question: Is it the homeowner's responsibility to warn visitors when they come into the house that there is an Alexa or a smart TV with a microphone that might be recording the conversations? Well,

Figure 7 *Does your house need this warning sign?*

maybe it is. For a client presentation I created the sign shown in Figure 7 to illustrate what a future home might be required to display at the front door.

In another case, a Middletown, Ohio, man, Ross Compton, narrowly escaped from a fire spreading through his home. He later told investigators that before he evacuated he grabbed a few things—the number turned out to be 15—including clothing and other personal effects packed into a couple of suitcases, his computer, and the charger for his smart pacemaker. Then he shattered a window with his cane, threw his bags outside, and exited the burning house. From the start, investigators were suspicious of anyone doing that much preparation when their house was on fire, and a witness had observed fire that appeared to be in several different parts of the house.

Finally, after investigators were granted a search warrant to access the medical data from Compton's pacemaker, they charged him with arson and insurance fraud. At a grand jury hearing, a cardiologist who reviewed the data testified that "it was highly improbable Mr. Compton would have been able to collect, pack, and remove the number of items from the house, exit his bedroom window, and carry numerous large and heavy items to the front of his residence during the short period of time he has indicated due to his medical conditions."

◻ ◻ ◻

A voice-driven digital assistant in your home. A pacemaker connected to the cloud transmitting data to a clinic. Your "smart" TV, fridge, baby monitor. The devices that are now part of the IoT were the stuff of science fiction only a couple of decades ago. Today, they're in our homes—and vulnerable. While few of us may be a suspect in a crime or accused of arson and insurance fraud, any of us could be the target of a hack.

One example is called a distributed denial of service (DDoS).

A DDoS is a kind of cyber attack where a botnet (a network of compromised systems programmed to send commands without the owners' knowledge) floods the bandwidth of a target system, like a server, overwhelming it with traffic until it collapses. The IoT might as well have been designed for hackers launching DDoS attacks. It has become a fad—everyone wants to jump on the bandwagon, throw a sensor or five into their products, and say they're part of the IoT. It's only possible to do that because of all the cheap-and-cheerful sensors that are available today. But just because something can be connected, should it be connected? It's not a good reason to do it just because it's modern and cool to be part of the IoT or just because you think everyone else is doing it.

Does it necessarily make sense to have sensors embedded in fridges, stoves, washing machines, dryers, coffeemakers, microwaves, robotic vacuum cleaners, toothbrushes, couches and chairs, baby monitors, home security systems, doorbells, lawn sprinklers, vibrators? Especially if there may be a security risk?

Let's look at a few examples. If you're elderly or very ill, staying in a hospital is an unpleasant thought (and considering the possible exposure to diseases and germs, also a potentially dangerous one). But if you had a nurse making regular house calls and a connected toilet performing analysis of urine and waste products, and sending that data to a doctor who is monitoring your condition, it could allow patients to spend much more time at home.

Also on the subject of health care, I read an interesting book, *The Patient Will See You Now: The Future of Medicine Is in Your Hands*, by Dr. Eric Topol. He talks about how digital health technology will revolutionize medicine and save lives. One example is a nano-sized sensor, with a wireless connection to your smartphone, that can be injected into the bloodstream to keep blood under continuous surveillance. Topol says that the sensor detects when endothelial cells, which have a unique genomic signal, are sloughed off an artery wall (a precursor to a heart attack). In such an event, a signal is then relayed to the smartphone, which alerts the patient to immediately call for medical assistance. And this doesn't necessarily need to be restricted to the coronary arteries. It could also be used for the cerebral arteries to pick up an early warning sign of a stroke.

This is very useful, even life-saving, stuff. But what businesses don't realize is the minute they add a sensor, they've made the transition from being a hardware company (ship-and-forget) that makes light bulbs or couches or microwaves or baby monitors, to a software company (ship-and-remember) that wraps its software in a light bulb, a couch, a baby monitor, or a microwave. That's a profound change. What are those sensors going to do?

Generate data. What are you planning to do with that data? Is the data secure? Is your software part of a robust security system? Can you patch or update your software the way software is updated on your computer or smartphone, or the way Tesla regularly updates the software on its cars?

Let's consider everyday uses. If you work outside your home, maybe it's convenient at the end of the day to open a smartphone app connected to your home thermostat and turn on the heat or central air so it's comfortable when you arrive home while saving utility costs during the day. Maybe it makes sense to be able to start your car and warm it up a few minutes before you get there (without unlocking the doors).

But what about a sensor in a sofa? What is it there for? (There is a model that makes noises to keep pets away.) If you're a manufacturer, are you prepared to make sure that sensor is secure and regularly being updated so it doesn't get hacked? Does your business model support the ability to regularly update the product "forever"?

So the question shouldn't be "Do I want to add sensors to my product?" It should be "Do I want to become a software company?" If a company can't answer yes to that question, it should not be participating in the IoT because it will probably be creating insecure products that can be leveraged by botnets to create cyber security threats.

Take, for example, the case of Brian Krebs.

In late September 2016, a massive DDoS attack on KrebsOnSecurity.com, the website of respected cyber security journalist Brian Krebs, forced his hosting company, Akamai Technologies, to remove him from its system. Krebs had been investigating DDoS attacks around the world, and his research on two Israeli hackers who ran a DDoS service-for-hire had led to their arrest, possibly prompting the attack. Within days, his website was up again thanks to Google's Project Shield, a free service offered to public service–related websites such as independent news outlets, human rights organizations, and election-monitoring sites that are vulnerable to DDoS attacks by those who want to censor them. It's easy to see how attacks like this could intimidate individuals.

But it's the implications of the Krebs attack that are important. It happened because of the proliferation of non-updateable, internet-connected devices that make up the IoT. In the past, botnets were commonly made up of a collection of computers. In Krebs's case, though, hackers had written a malware program called Mirai, which scanned the internet looking for insecure IoT systems with easy-to-bypass, factory-default usernames and passwords: security cameras, routers, digital video recorders, and the like. Then, like a slave army, Mirai commanded a botnet comprising hundreds of thousands of devices to send an incredible volume of traffic—estimated at 600 to 700 giga-bits per second—to Krebs's site, overwhelming it. Mirai is exceptionally dangerous because it lurks on devices that users seldom think about or deal with—they typically have no idea their webcam, security camera, or router is part of a botnet.

I've talked about open source quite a bit in this book. Here's how it can be used for destructive purposes: Shortly after attacking Krebs's site, the creator of the Mirai malware released the source code on an internet hackers' forum so any hacker could use it and even make changes to create different strains to be used for more attacks.

A month later, Mirai was responsible for another, even larger, DDoS attack directed at Dyn, a firm responsible for a significant portion of the internet's domain name infrastructure (sometimes thought of as a kind of "switch-board"), forcing companies as diverse as Amazon, Twitter, Airbnb, Comcast, Netflix, PayPal, Spotify, Starbucks, Verizon Communications, CNN, *The New York Times*, and *The Wall Street Journal* to shut down. If a DDoS attack can do this much damage, it could potentially do more serious damage to government infrastructure or even disrupt an election.

Later, when the Mirai attacks were analyzed by cyber security firm Flashpoint Intel, they had one common ele-ment—a majority of the compromised devices (mainly DVRs and surveillance cameras) contained components from one

Chinese manufacturer: XiongMai Technologies, based in Hangzhou. The devices are inexpensive, with default usernames and passwords that are easy for malware to crack. Worse, the password is hardcoded and there are no tools available to disable it. Moreover, owing to the inexpensive nature of the devices, they cannot be software updated.

While this might all be news to many people, it's been common knowledge within the tech world that the IoT represents a disaster waiting to happen. In January 2015, Edith Ramirez, chairperson of the U.S. Federal Trade Commission, called on delegates at the Consumer Electronics Show in Las Vegas—not all of whom wanted to hear the message—to do more to address privacy.

> *Data security is already challenging, as evidenced by the growing number of high-profile breaches with which we are all familiar. But security in an IoT world is likely to present unique challenges. As an initial matter, some of the developers entering the IoT market, unlike hardware and software companies, have not spent decades thinking about how to secure their products and services from hackers. And, the small size and limited processing power of many connected devices could inhibit encryption and other robust security measures. Moreover, some connected devices are low-cost and essentially disposable. If a vulnerability is discovered*

on that type of device, it may be difficult to update the software or apply a patch—or even to get news of a fix to consumers...

That is the problem. Consumers want a webcam and, as long as it works, they want the cheapest one they can buy. They don't notice when malware hijacks just a little bit of their webcam services from them, along with a little bit from many others, to create a botnet. At most they might notice a small degradation of service, but if it essentially has no impact on them, what incentive is there for them to pay more for a webcam with better, more secure sensors? And why would the Chinese manufacturer want to reduce its margins by equipping its product with more expensive, better-secured sensors when the customer is not demanding it?

That's why the Mirai botnet is so scary—it takes advantage of cheap-and-cheerful IoT hardware, and there's nothing that can be done unless people start demanding that their products be secured. I discussed this in 2017 during a talk I gave to the insurance industry. "The insurance industry," I said, "should be tracking companies that build software-based products like DVRs, webcams, thermostats, cars and all the other 'things' out there to understand their software lifecycle management." I suggested that the insurance industry should be asking whether or not the companies continually update their software as they learn of vulnerabilities. If not, then the customers should be charged a higher premium for products that are not "insurance approved." This way, pure economic forces will change the behavior of companies.

Mirai isn't the first malware to be unleashed by hackers nor will it be the last. It just became a high-profile symbol of the IoT's vulnerability. What was supposed to be progress—the ability to have home products communicate with each other—to be able to remotely change a thermostat setting, turn on an oven, find out what's in your fridge—has turned out to be a hacker's paradise.

Let's consider a really chilling scenario: "smart" baby products. Aside from baby monitors connected to smartphone apps and motion detectors, there are blankets, booties, and even an entire garment with sensors that transmit to a phone a baby's heart rate, temperature, and oxygen levels, and even records when the baby rolls over. Aside from distracting parents from being attentive to natural cues, some products can cause rashes. But more importantly, are the sensors secure and receiving software updates to protect against the latest hacking trends? What if sensors were hacked to, say, cause the temperature to be reduced or increased, and you didn't notice until too late? That's an extreme example, of course, but not outside the realm of possibility.

I've done consulting for many different companies, and I often give executives a wake-up call about the IoT.

While doing some work for a window and door company—I'll call it ACME Products—I met with members of the executive team. I showed them a newspaper article with a headline that read "Woman assaulted and killed, children slaughtered. ACME Products implicated." Of course, I had faked it to make a point. They were annoyed and told me I didn't understand.

"We just make doors and windows," they said. "If someone picks a lock or shatters a window, we are not to blame."

"At one time, you'd have been right. But today you're selling what you advertise as a smart door, and the carpenter who installed that smart door didn't understand how they work. He left the door set to default so it was never properly locked, which means you're implicated. When you began installing sensors and marketing smart doors, you became a software company, and now you have new obligations," I replied.

They didn't want to hear it, but they knew I was right.

My story also illustrates why, if companies aren't required to do so, it's up to consumers to assume new responsibilities for their security.

When we rent a car, the first thing most of us do is pair it with our smartphone. Sometimes the first thing that pops up on the infotainment center's screen is data from previous renters. When returning the car, often in a rush, how many of us remember to delete our personal data? If we don't, we're leaving a digital trail for anyone to trace—addresses, phone numbers, call logs, locations visited—and there is no regulation requiring rental car companies to do it themselves.

Sometimes, people elect to simply reject the new technology. It's possible to avoid pairing a phone with a rental car's system. To listen to music from your device, you can use an auxiliary cable to connect the headphone port on your phone directly into the infotainment system. If the car has a cigarette lighter adapter, a phone can be charged using that rather than a USB port, and a Bluetooth kit for multiple devices works for hand's-free calling.

Companies can opt out, too. In January 2017, a four-star Austrian hotel, the Seehotel Jaegerwirt, was attacked by hackers who compromised computers, encrypting data that prevented staff from programming keycards for incoming guests. It was the fourth time the hotel had been targeted and, once again, the company's IT service paid a ransom in Bitcoin. A spokesperson from the hotel confirmed that the Seehotel Jaegerwirt would be switching back to old-fashioned keys.

❏ ❏ ❏

I have done some consulting for a major North American oil and gas company that derives 40% of its revenues from dispensing gas and 40% from the sale of goods and services in its convenience stores. (Refining represents the other 20%.) I sat in a boardroom with about a dozen executives. We began talking about its network of gasoline stations with retail convenience stores. I asked if they'd been preparing for the autonomous car and truck revolution. There seemed to be quite a few blank faces so I pointed out that Ford has announced a fully autonomous vehicle by 2021, and that Otto, Uber's recently acquired start-up, retrofits semi-trucks with radars, cameras, and laser sensors and will soon have self-driving fleets on the highways. In the fall of 2016, an Otto-equipped truck loaded with 50,000 cans of Budweiser drove 120 miles, from Fort Collins to Colorado Springs, CO, without human control.

Everyone expects the first use of autonomous vehicles will be for fleets—taxis, couriers, trucking companies—rather than individual consumers. During this transition period, fleet owners can first operate locally, keeping strict control of their vehicles, including maintenance, and hacks are less likely to happen when access to the vehicles is restricted to authorized employees.

I suggested to the oil and gas executives that we leave the trend toward electrical vehicles out of the equation for the moment and simply discuss gas-powered but autonomous vehicles. Oil and gas companies have, for years, spent a great deal of time and money advertising—through signage, radio and TV commercials, loyalty cards, and discount offers—to people like me, a human driver, hoping we will feel emotionally tied to buying gas at their stations. With gas-powered but autonomous vehicles, who would make the decision about where to get gas? A lot of the stops vehicles make are for the convenience of a driver (or by law, since truck drivers can't drive for more than a restricted number of hours). Autonomous vehicles will need to make fewer stops since without drivers there will be room for larger gas tanks.

Autonomous vehicles with combustion engines will still need gas, but now the challenge for oil and gas companies will be identifying and influencing the decision-makers at the autonomous fleet's headquarters, because it's likely they will choose one gas provider for the entire fleet. And even if you win the contract with a fleet so its vehicles stop at your stations—or perhaps deliver bulk gas to the fleet's headquarters—what happens to the profitable retail shops when there's no driver? Oh, and the entire strategy behind gas station locations was based on people driving vehicles. Do the locations still make sense when more and more autonomous vehicles are on the road?

At least with gas-powered cars there's an opportunity to lobby fleet owners to stop at your stations. What about electric cars? This is a different issue, since it's not necessarily related to autonomy. Tesla has a firm place in the market and has recently released its moderately priced Tesla 3. The Chevy Bolt, which can get 200 miles on a full-charged battery, is on the market. In 2017, Ford announced that it will offer 13 electrified vehicles—both hybrids and fully electric models—within the next 5 years, and Mercedes and Volkswagen plan to launch all-electric cars in 2019. Audi will soon market an all-electric luxury sedan and SUV, and there will also be offerings from Nissan, Hyundai, and Volvo.

Looking into the faces of the executives, I asked what plans they'd made to respond to what will soon be a growing number of electric vehicles. Have they been talking to Tesla and the executives in charge of the electric programs at the big automakers? Have they been thinking about retrofitting their outlets with charging stations? Drivers can plug their electric cars in at home and charge them overnight, so for relatively short distances they probably won't need to re-charge. But for longer trips outside of cities, on business, for example, or when taking vacations, they will likely have to re-charge. Do your locations still make sense for the electric car model? How do you market yourself to these drivers? Are you offering the best charging stations? The fastest? The cheapest?

These profound changes to our world affect businesses of every kind. If you look inside a fully autonomous car, many things we all expect to see aren't there: a driver's seat, a steering wheel, gas and brake pedals, a dashboard. And since there's no driver, there's no radio. Even when we have autonomous passenger cars, passengers will pair their smartphones and listen to whatever they're accustomed to listening to when they're not in their car, as the majority of people still driving cars do now. So why include a radio in a car?

That's a complexity the National Association of Broadcasters (NAB) is thinking about. NAB is a trade association and lobby group representing over-the-air radio and TV broadcasters in the U.S. Is there a way to create an incentive for automakers to continue equipping over-the-air radios in their vehicles? What if NAB offered to flow a percentage of the advertising dollars to the automakers, giving them a reason to remain involved? A smaller percentage of something is better than 100% of nothing.

The IoT doesn't only affect urban centers. Its impact on farming is going to be huge. In some cases, the benefits are obvious. A smart farm might have soil moisture sensors that alert farmers to the need for fungicides or drainage valves that control watering of fields. Bio-monitoring devices could monitor temperature, respiration, heart rate, and other vital signs to evaluate livestock health. Farm machinery giant John Deere has "smart" tractors and combines that can control how many seeds are planted per acre, precisely how far apart they're planted, and the pressure on each seed (corresponding to the softness of the soil). One product replaces a tractor's steering wheel with a device that can make turns within an accuracy of about an inch.

However, one IoT issue in particular is upsetting the farming community. In 2015, a battle emerged between farmers and John Deere over the ability to repair farm equipment. For generations, farmers have repaired their own equipment. Now, agricultural equipment is becoming so high-tech that, like the newest cars, access to elaborate manuals, patented diagnostic tools, licensed technologists, and proprietary parts are required to fix them.

Farmers were especially angered by John Deere's stipulation forbidding all repairs and modifications to equipment and preventing farmers from suing for "crop loss, lost profits, loss of goodwill, loss of use of equipment … arising from the performance or non-performance of any aspect of the software." That meant only John Deere dealerships and authorized repair shops could work on the newest equipment. In fact, the company tried to stipulate that farmers don't even own the equipment for which they paid hundreds of thousands of dollars. Instead, they purchased an "implied license for the life of the vehicle to operate that vehicle." It makes it nearly impossible for the person who purchases a product containing software to access that software.

Given the seasonal and time restrictions on farming, waiting for an authorized dealer who might be 200 miles away to come to your farm to fix a broken-down tractor could mean the difference between success and bankruptcy. It's no wonder many farmers have been forced to act like criminals, seeking out black market manuals, parts, and software.

Farmers have banned together in protest, calling for a "right to repair" bill that would force manufacturers, like John Deere, to provide customers and independent repair shops with authorized service manuals, tools, and parts. As of this writing, this kind of legislation is being considered in eight U.S. states (Nebraska, Minnesota, Massachusetts, New York, Illinois, Wyoming, Tennessee, and Kansas).

While this example is a major problem for the farming community, it has implications for the entire IoT. Do we own what we buy or simply lease the use of someone else's software? We are already looking at a time when mechanics will no longer be able to order cheaper aftermarket parts for cars. The physical part can be replicated, but how that part functions is controlled by software.

The IoT is not going away, and the current business model for the IoT is not working. It's clear we will need government regulations to fix it.

YOUR DATA IN WHOSE HANDS?

T he premise of the *Zero Dollar Car* is built on a key foundation: We, as consumers, should have control of our personal data. But we don't. Today's business models provide us with "free" access to content, services, and things (things that often contain sensors for which the utility is modest, at best) in exchange for our data. On March 17, 2017, the 28th birthday of the world wide web, Sir Tim Berners-Lee, the founder of the web, wrote:

As our data is then held in proprietary silos, out of sight to us, we lose out on the benefits we could realize if we had direct control over this data and chose when, and with whom, to share it. What's more, we often do not have any way of feeding back to companies what data we'd rather not share...

And there's an unprecedented avalanche of data out there. At one time, it was mainly our emails and search engine activity. Then came texts and social media. Today, it's everything from our smartphone's GPS signals to the IP addresses of our toasters and security systems to our Fitbits or implantable sensors monitoring heart valves, with more "things" coming each and every day. All of it generating data that's being scrutinized by data refineries' algorithms—analyzed, combined, sorted, processed. According to the May 6, 2017, issue of *The Economist*, "Data are to this century what oil was to the last one: a driver of growth and change." That's why a small, but enormously data-driven automaker like Tesla is valued higher than the much larger GM.

What does all this mean to you and me?

In this book I've outlined some very serious implications of big data. The IoT made possible, in part, the May 2017 WannaCry ransomware hack that infected more than 200,000 systems in 150 countries and caused global havoc,

crippling transportation systems and hospitals and shut-
ting down ATMs. While disruptive, it was also amateurish,
but it illustrated how vulnerable the world is, especially
when more sophisticated hackers mount a more effective
attack in the future.

Another notable example: In September 2016, Yahoo
revealed that at least 500 million user accounts had been
hacked. What's worse, we later learned that the hack
itself happened in 2014, which meant the hackers had
access to all of that data for *nearly two years*! In case you
thought Yahoo's reputation couldn't be more tarnished, in
December 2016, the technology company admitted that
another hack had taken place in 2013 involving the data
of *1 billion* users.

But the problem isn't just hackers. Here's another
example that created a viral storm but shows just how
confusing these issues can be today. Early in 2010, *The
New York Times Magazine* ran a long feature article called
"How Companies Learn Your Secrets." In it, the writer
discussed the field of "predictive analytics"—a term that
means applying to data the use of statistical algorithms
and machine learning to identify the likelihood of future
outcomes. In business, it's used to crunch data to pre-
dict consumer purchases before they happen. The article
told a story of an anonymous father who came to his
local Target outside Minneapolis complaining that his

high-school-aged daughter had received coupons from the company for maternity clothing and nursery furniture. According to the article, he angrily asked, "Are you trying to encourage her to get pregnant?"

When the store's manager looked into it, he discovered the teenager had received the mailings from Target. When he called the father again to apologize, the father admitted he had not been told that his daughter was, indeed, pregnant.

After a follow-up article in *Forbes* ran with the headline "How Target Figured Out a Teen Girl Was Pregnant Before Her Father Did," the rest of the media piled on, leading to a public relations nightmare for Target. The story—that a Target statistician had developed a "pregnancy-prediction" model based on women's past purchases—struck people as devious if not creepy. Since then, doubts have been raised about whether the "pregnancy-prediction" model was actually successful, or whether Target would focus on a demographic of women who hadn't revealed their pregnancy, or whether the teenager may have just been accidentally slotted into the wrong marketing segment.

In any event, *The New York Times Magazine* article showed that Target's marketing analytics department at least explored all kinds of data-driven possibilities to better assess when customers—including pregnant ones—were ready to buy, and that the public (and the media) is inclined to believe the worst in any company when it comes to data collection.

As journalist and technology activist Cory Doctorow wrote in 2015, "The IoT's would-be architects share a common belief: that 'people' are just another kind of 'thing,' and that you serve people by acting on their behalf, by anticipating them, asking their personal network for important facts about them, and then adapting the world around them in real time to provide the magic."

I've argued that there are two fundamental changes that should happen if we are to fully achieve the societal benefits of "big data":

1. **Companies need to transition from a ship-and-forget product culture to a ship-and-remember one.**

    Businesses need to take responsibility for the software integrated into their products and provide regular and timely updates, especially patches when vulnerabilities are discovered. Every company that includes sensors in its products is, by default, a software company. That's what Ford was so slow to accept when I worked there, and what other companies that I work with today generally fail to understand. The result, I would argue, contributed to Ford's declining market share and stock market performance, which led to a shake-up in May of 2017. CEO Mark Fields, whom I once coached on the future of technology, was replaced by a former member of Ford's board of directors with a reputation for crisis management.

2. Society needs to redefine the concept of ownership.

This is at the heart of the IoT. With so much software in so many places—even including what we wear—the question of who owns the data is becoming critical. We all leave a digital trail wherever we go, and so far, every time we click "accept" on one of those long, confusing terms-and-conditions forms that no one reads, we give away our personal data—a priceless asset not only to marketers but corporations and governments. What do we get in return? "Free" email, text, internet search, and content. And we also give up our data every time we order a product on Amazon or Target, accept a discount from a travel company or airline, purchase a new appliance or home security system, pair our smartphone with our car...

Do we really surrender our data so readily because we believe we get a fair return in benefits?

That's what we've been led to believe, especially by marketers, but I often doubted it. Then, in 2015, a survey conducted by the University of Pennsylvania's Annenberg School for Communication confirmed my instincts. Titled "The Tradeoff Fallacy: How Marketers Are Misrepresenting American Consumers and Opening Them Up to Exploitation," the survey contacted a representative sample of 1506 Americans over 18 years of age who use the internet or email "at least occasionally." Their key findings:

- 91% (77% of them strongly) disagree that "if companies give me a discount, it is a fair exchange for them to collect information about me without my knowing."
- 71% (53% of them strongly) disagree that "it's fair for an online or physical store to monitor what I'm doing online when I'm there, in exchange for letting me use the store's wireless internet, or Wi-Fi, without charge."
- 55% (38% of them strongly) disagree that "it's okay if a store where I shop uses information it has about me to create a picture of me that improves the services they provide me."

The report goes on to say that "further analysis of these responses indicate only a very small percentage of Americans agree with the overall concept of trade-offs. In fact, only about 4% agree or agree strongly with all three propositions."

Furthermore, "58% agreed with both of the following two statements that together indicate resignation: 'I want to have control over what marketers know about me online' and 'I've come to accept that I have little control over what marketers can learn about me online'."

This study perfectly captures the thrust of *The Zero Dollar Car*. Anyone who uses email or Facebook, drives a connected car or engages in any of the thousands of other data-gathering actions resigns themselves to their fate. Why? Because the average person can't see how they could stop Google, Facebook, Ford, or the myriad companies that build such products.

Is there any way to profit from our personal data? A few enterprising individuals have been trying. The London-based CitizenMe launched in 2014 to help average people take control of their personal data. Similar to the privacyfix.com utility I discussed back in Chapter 1, the idea was to show consumers that the data they were sharing publicly on their various social media networks was being collected, analyzed, and used for profit by others. As it turns out, that's pretty complicated, and the app never broke through to a mass market. However, there was one very popular feature: a Facebook personality test. So, in 2016, the company partnered with the University of Sheffield's Open Data Science Institute to reboot itself as a market research and big data analysis service, still driven by CitizenMe's original principle: that personal data should work on behalf of users, not exploited by for-profit corporations that don't necessarily care about the rights of individual users.

Another start-up, called Datacoup, described itself as a "personal data marketplace." It's a New York-based data-mining firm with an unusual twist: In exchange for providing personal data, such as social media information and credit card information, individuals are paid a monthly fee of $8 U.S. Consumers received some compensation for their data and were also able to specify which data, and how much, they shared through Datacoup.

Returning to the Zero Dollar Car concept, some start-ups are helping the automakers—not individuals—monetize data. An Israeli firm called Otonomo connects carmakers and drivers with service providers, like dealerships, insurance companies, and even, theoretically, smart cities, to optimize the profitability of all the data a vehicle is producing. And another Israeli start-up, Nexar, has developed a dashboard app using drivers' smartphones that will, once enough people are using it, provide real-time, vehicle-to-vehicle information that could alert users to slowdowns ahead (so they can plan around them) or even an accident in the process of happening a few cars ahead (so drivers have a chance to react). That could be a valuable service for drivers, and it relieves automakers of a data-collecting function that's time consuming and expensive. But, of course, Nexar's system is old-school in one way: Once you sign up, your data is available to Nexar to sell to third parties.

I believe some kind of system that allows individuals to have a share in monetizing their data is the way we need to go. If we, as consumers, don't understand how much data we generate or how to measure it—if we don't understand how it's stored, processed, and used to drive profits—we lose. To win, we should be paid compensation for that data (the plan on which CitizenMe based its original idea) or receive a big reduction in the price of the product or service involved (the Zero Dollar Car model).

Will individual consumers, like you or me, ever be able to monetize the sensors in our vehicle the way I outline in the Zero Dollar Car? Right now, it remains an opportunity waiting to happen. Google, Apple, and other corporations don't want to do business that way. They prefer to do multimillion-dollar deals with brands.

So the challenge for individuals is to truly understand that this world of data exists and that it only exists because their personal data is being transacted, often without their knowledge or permission. Once consumers understand that, they can begin to agitate for some kind of control over their data, or even government involvement. What they should expect is a contract that outlines the precise dollar figure they will receive in return for their data.

That's why, in most of my engagements today, I educate clients on what I call the "big red button" business model. In essence, that is the ability, when you purchase or use any digitally enabled product or service, to opt in or opt out. With the opt-in choice, consumers pay less—"zero," or at least a substantially reduced price—in exchange for their data. They have, essentially, bartered away their privacy. If instead they opt to hit the "big red button," all of their data will be destroyed and non-recoverable (called "the right to be forgotten," it's a practice formally adopted in the European Union and Argentina), but they will pay full price in exchange for privacy.

This business solution for building products will never happen until the "big red button"—which we could also think of as a way of turning privacy into a commodity, or the "right to be forgotten"—is enshrined in law and there is a regulatory body enforcing it.

Writing *The Zero Dollar Car* has been an interesting journey. It's my attempt—along with people like Cory Doctorow, Electronic Frontier Foundation, Kyle Wiens, and Clive Thompson—to raise awareness about the bigger issues embroiled in privacy and software. Big issues that we all face. It's only when we're armed with knowledge about where our personal data is going and how it's being used that we can truly understand the scope of our opportunities and creatively act on them, if that's our choice.

I hope you've enjoyed the ride.

ACKNOWLEDGMENTS

M y deepest thanks to the following people for their support and guidance.

The editorial, production, and creative team who worked on this book, including David, Tracy, Zoja, Natalie, and Kyle. A special thanks to Sarah Scott of Barlow Books, who originally suggested my Zero Dollar Car idea was a book.

Edward Peck from Asset Finance International for giving me stage time in London to first develop the *Zero Dollar Car* storyline.

Kevin Gutzmer, whose friendship has been long standing and who conceived and developed the analysis behind the original digital life worth question.

Richard Windsor from Radio Free Mobile, whose economic study of ecosystems provides continuous information and value and underpinning to the Zero Dollar Car concept.

Brother Gerard Brereton, who launched me on the path I am today and has been a significant force in my life.

La familia Bayón. Gracias por todo el amor y apoyo. Ustedes han tocado significativamente mi vida.

Mom and Dad. Thank you for a wonderful upbringing and the love and attention you showed. You are the reason I am what I am today.

My brothers and sisters. If you hadn't pushed on that St. Patrick's day, I wouldn't have gone to Reilly's and life would be very different today.

My children. Kate, Ciara, Kelli, and John, thanks for putting up with the many hours of work and computer time and continuing to ask me to play. You are the light of my world.

My bride. Karen, thanks for saying yes and being there every day since. I love you more than words can say.

INDEX

ABOUT THE AUTHOR

Photo credit: Karen Ellis

John Ellis is an author and expert in big data. As a big data futurist, John articulates actionable outcomes for the new and yet unseen business models of the world's leading sectors like transportation, insurance, telecommunications, government, and home. John speaks around the world about how data—from cars and all kinds of devices—will transform industries, business models, and our lives. He was the global technologist and head of the Ford Developer Program with Ford Motor Company. Previous to that, he was an executive with Motorola delivering wireless software products and services to the mobile industry.

John can be found online at **www.johntellis.com**.